Dear Lord James
A Critique of Teacher Education
Edited by Tyrrell Burgess

Penguin Books

Penguin Books Ltd, Harmondsworth,
Middlesex, England
Penguin Books Inc., 7110 Ambassador Road,
Baltimore, Md 21207, U.S.A.
Penguin Books Australia Ltd,
Ringwood, Victoria, Australia

First published 1971
Copyright © Tyrrell Burgess and contributors, 1971

Made and printed in Great Britain by
Hazell Watson & Viney Ltd,
Aylesbury, Bucks
Set in Linotype Times

Penguin Education

Penguin Education Specials
General Editor: Willem van der Eyken

M. J. Mart
July 197
Norwich

Dear Lord James
A Critique of Teacher Education
Edited by Tyrrell Burgess

Contents

Introduction

Dear Lord James

You have been asked by the Secretary of State for Education
and Science to chair an expert committee undertaking an
intensive short inquiry into teacher education. You were
appointed not a moment too soon. Of course the colleges of
education, where most teachers are trained, have just been
through an unprecedented expansion, and their staffs have until
recently felt, with earlier Secretaries of State, that a full-scale
inquiry would be something of a last straw. On the other hand,
there is long-standing dissatisfaction both in the schools and
among the students in the colleges about the direction and
quality of teacher education, and there is growing debate about
the role of the colleges and their place in higher education. Not
that the criticism and debate come only from outside: some of
the most searching questions are from inside the colleges. The
object of this book is to draw your special attention to some of
the problems and to suggest priorities.

Our concern begins, of course, not so much with colleges or
student teachers, but with the schools and with the children in
them. Whenever we discuss teacher education we should be
thinking primarily of the six year old learning to read, the
eleven year old embarking on unfamiliar subjects, or the young
adult seeking qualifications for a job or further education.
Judged by all the normal external measures, some of the work
of schools and teachers is relatively impressive. Standards of
reading have been rising since the war, and continue to rise.
More and more pupils are gaining success in external examinations. More and more are staying on voluntarily at school and
going on to further and higher education. In an important sense
this represents a vote of confidence in teachers and their
training.

At the same time, teachers are personally taking increasing
professional responsibility. For example, the new methods in

education based upon treating each child as an individual have been spreading gradually through the primary schools and into the secondary stage. This process has been almost wholly due to the work of teachers. Again, the new Certificate of Secondary Education is controlled by teachers, and one of its three 'modes' of operation gives individual teachers and their schools the chance and the encouragement to create their own syllabuses and examinations.

But this is not all. Society at large is making its own demands, and these are becoming increasingly pressing. We should not underestimate the burden which social change imposes. A society which is becoming more democratic and less authoritarian places particular strains on the teacher–pupil relationship. A society which needs increasing technical skill and competence makes heavy demands on the education service. Every year we are expecting more of our children, more of our schools and more of our teachers.

Of course many different people and organizations have a hand in meeting these demands. You do not need to be reminded of the overall responsibility of the Department of Education and Science, nor of the role of the local education authorities in providing schools in their areas. Individual schools are finding solutions to their own particular problems. But clearly what happens in education depends to an enormous extent on what happens when an individual teacher meets a particular class. Education is a personal service: it succeeds or fails with people, not with systems. What the authorities can do is to remove inhibitions, to set a framework which actually encourages individual teachers and pupils to give of their best.

It is because a group of us have been convinced that educational change depends so much upon the individual teacher that we have founded a 'Society for the Promotion of Educational Reform through Teacher Training'. SPERTTT began as a protest, a protest first against the inadequate experience, despite improvement, of most children in our schools. We believed reform was vital – but however much the Inspectorate may advise, the Schools Council publish, the DES suggest, or the LEAs withhold or dispense, none of these seemed likely to enrich the provision in schools or the experience of children unless the classroom teachers were adequately trained and prepared.

So our protest was directed at this most sensitive area of the educational cycle – at the point where teachers are made. We knew well enough that the preparation of teachers was no simple process, that the expansion of the last ten years had been too much of a good thing and that the whole field was thick with contradictory problems. But we felt that we must attack.

We haven't ourselves had the resources to mount a full-scale inquiry. Most of us believed this was necessary and have urged successive Governments to establish one. But even without such an inquiry there was much evidence we could rely upon, much that could be collected by volunteers. We appealed, therefore, for members – and we were joined by a host of supporters from all over the country – to mount local study groups, arrange conferences, examine special facets of teacher preparation, with a view to publicizing and disseminating good practices, and in order to incite those responsible for preparing teachers to think critically, and to act radically in pursuit of improvement.

One of the special advantages enjoyed by SPERTTT has been that our membership, while being drawn mainly from people teaching in colleges and departments of education, includes a large number of teachers in schools, students in training, parents, administrators and councillors, and many others interested in the reform of education through teacher training. This book has grown out of some of our discussions – though we ought to make clear that some of its contributors are less committed to the Society than others. The book is not so much a SPERTTT manifesto as an attempt by the Society to put together a radical critique of teacher education as a contribution to the debate at large, and in particular to your inquiry.

To put it baldly, there are three main complaints about teacher training as it now exists. The first is that in social terms it is a failure. We know that the students in colleges of education, like students in universities, are socially homogeneous. They come, on the whole, from middle-class families – at least very few of their parents are manual workers, skilled or un-skilled (and those who have such parents soon adopt an attitude and style indistinguishable from the rest). Their experience of education has been typically success at 11-plus and grammar school. In other words, their background and education are quite different from those of most children, indeed from those of the children they themselves will be teaching. It is now clear that this fact distorts the attitudes of teachers to their pupils and the expectations they have of pupils' performance. The amusing study by Rosenthal and Jackson in California, which showed how children chosen at random, but about whom predictions of 'intellectual blooming' had been made, duly bloomed, has been paralleled by research in England showing how teacher expectations affect pupils' performance. The com-plaint about teacher education today is that it does too little to free teachers from the presuppositions of their background and too little to help them positively to understand the social con-text in which they and their pupils are working.

The second complaint about teacher education is that it is academic and remote from reality. We must be careful not to be too critical about this. Up to a point, one would expect the training of teachers to be inappropriate for schools as they are. One of the purposes of teacher education is, after all, to change the practice of the schools. Many of the sneers from older teachers about the impracticability of training derive from nothing more serious than an instinctive defence of their own conservatism. But this in a way reinforces the point. If the newly trained teacher is likely to encounter difficulties or even opposition, his training must offer more than radical attitudes and good intentions: it must be a training in meeting, first, the obstacles he is likely to encounter and, second, the intellectual challenge of new methods. Many young teachers find, not that their ideas are inappropriate but that their train-ing has ignored some of the most obvious practical skills which a teacher needs – like how to achieve order in a difficult school.

They also find that it has neglected to give them the intel-lectual and practical means to cope with new educational demands. It may be that the teaching profession as a whole can claim credit for new approaches in maths and science, for rethinking the education of the adolescent for a higher school-leaving age, for introducing such ideas as diagnostic teaching, the integrated day and family grouping, for trying and evaluating new approaches to reading. But it is probably true that most teachers, indeed most young teachers, find themselves in all this quite as bewildered as parents. There is much experiment without understanding. One of the incidental results of greater parent–teacher cooperation has been to reveal that most teachers are unable to give a clear and coherent defence of what they and the schools are trying to do, except in the most general and bland terms. This is because the college of education courses have failed to evolve a properly understood vocational education at a high intellectual level.

This raises the third major complaint about teacher education – that it lacks rigour. It is not just that the failure rate is suspiciously low, not just that student teachers find themselves covering similar ground to that which they tramped over at A-level, not just that some of the practical work is often appropriate for seven year olds. It is that the course as a whole offers too little intellectual challenge. The evidence which we offer in Chapters 1 and 2 of this book will surprise few people in education, even though we believe that Chapter 1 has an immediacy and Chapter 2 a comprehensiveness which give them an added value.

These, then, are the three major complaints about teacher education. We do not labour them. The bulk of our book is devoted to constructive suggestions for reform. Its second part seeks to cure the malaise revealed in the first. It considers the values of teacher education and suggests how it is possible to build on what is valuable in the traditions of the college. It then goes on to offer a curriculum for teacher education. Here the recommendations are quite specific. We believe that the structure and content of courses should be based on clear objectives. The curriculum needs to be conceived in relation to a knowledge-based, rationally constituted teaching profession, in which unity arises through diversity of function. The general principle underlying it is that all academic study should be viewed within the professional frame of reference. We are quite clear in wishing to reduce the academic and social isolation of the colleges. The recommendations for the detailed curriculum are rooted in what we take to be the future needs of the schools, and they imply a much closer relationship than hitherto between educational theory, subject specialization and educational practice. Our suggestions for doing this centre round a strengthened relationship between schools and colleges. We accept the need for a well-considered teacher–tutor system based on schools, and we seek a coherent system involving schools, teacher centres and colleges, in which initial training, the probationary year and in-service education offer a total and continuing form of teacher education.

The third part of the book contains what we believe to be its most distinctive contribution. This is because it tackles the institutional implications of educational proposals. What we seek to discuss is how policy can be implemented. We lay emphasis on this because we fear that the work of your committee will be hampered – through no fault of its own – by the way in which it was established. There may be some fields where the appointment of a small, full-time and expert committee could produce a powerful and influential report, but without disrespect to you and your colleagues we feel bound to question the relevance of your expertise. Teacher training is not something where a powerful group of people can discover the truth very quickly and make convincing and acceptable proposals. There are many ways of training teachers, many good ways, and in an important sense it does not matter which one a group of 'experts' pronounces to be the best.

More important, teacher training is pre-eminently a political area. To be sure it is not a matter of party politics, but there are many different interests involved, all of them quite legitimate, which have to be reconciled. The Secretary of State, the local authorities, the teachers' associations, and staff and students in the colleges, the nation at large represented by parental, industrial and other pressure groups – all these have a legitimate interest in what happens in teacher education. Will the kind of inquiry you have been asked to conduct allow time for the formulation and expression of these interests?

There is an even more cogent objection. The whole education service, including those engaged in teacher education, has come to see that change is inevitable here. But there has been very little agreement about the direction it should take. This circumstance cried out for a full-scale inquiry of the old-fashioned advisory council kind. Such an inquiry not only sets in train its own research projects and through its own discussions represents in a rough and ready way the attitude of informed public opinion; it also sets off a debate in public among those chiefly concerned. By the time a central advisory council reports, its recommendations tend to come as no surprise and are regarded as broadly acceptable. This is their great virtue. What happens is that through the public debate and discussion new proposals become acceptable and change can take place by consent. In short, the full-scale public inquiry is an essential instrument of democratic government.

One can think of two inquiries, one an example, the other an awful warning to you – both from higher education. The great and accepted achievement of the Robbins Committee was to make acceptable the idea of expansion to an academic community which had been more than reluctant to contemplate it. This achievement rested much less upon the actual report, even with all those appendixes, than it did on the fact that the argument went on for the two years in which the committee sat and the expansionist case could be clearly seen to be the better.

Compare this with the work of the Prices and Incomes Board on academic salaries. Here, too, the objective of the Board was to change university attitudes, particularly to notions of productivity. Its members were expert and they worked quickly. They reported twice. On the issues they themselves regarded as important they carried no conviction and commanded no assent. This is quite simply because the people concerned had no share in the formulation of objectives and in the creation of consensus. The danger is that your own inquiry will likewise lack the time and organization to engender widespread and acceptable change. You could easily produce a trendy consultants' report which no doubt will be elegant, rational and dead.

Nor are you much helped by your terms of reference, which are to inquire into the present arrangements for the education, training and probation of teachers in England and Wales 'in the light of the review currently being undertaken by the Area Training Organizations and of the evidence published by the former Select Committee on Education and Science'. Mention of these two other forms of inquiry was no doubt a ministerial courtesy. The Area Training Organizations were supposed to have reported by now on the action they had taken as a result of their own reviews – but it appears that their initial reports will not be available until autumn 1971, when you ought to be busy drafting. The Select Committee never quite decided what the purpose of its inquiry was, so it is not at all clear what the volumes of its collected evidence signify.

But your terms of reference ask you in particular to examine what the content and organization of courses should be; whether more intending teachers should be educated with students either bound for other careers or undecided; and what should be the role of the colleges of education, the polytechnics, other FE colleges and universities. 'And to make recommendations.'

These terms of reference are both specific and wide ranging, so it is fascinating to notice what you have *not* been asked to examine. You have not been asked to examine the future role of teachers. This is a large topic, and may have been thought to be incompatible with a quick inquiry. Equally, you have not been asked to examine the demand for teachers. The old National Advisory Council, which was slighted and then killed by the Department, was at least confronted by its terms of reference with the truth that the training and supply of teachers are intimately linked. Nor have you been asked to consider the place of teacher training within higher education. But the colleges of education not only supply the schools with teachers: they also provide, especially for girls, an important opportunity for higher education. You would be in less difficulty if there were some known Government policy for the size and balance of higher education. But there isn't one.

Because you have been asked to report at breakneck speed, you may have to limit the work which you take on, confining yourself to your terms of reference. This means that you may have to make *assumptions* about these questions which need

fundamental debate. You may have to assume that the role of
the teacher is to stay much as it is, that the numbers required
and the future size of higher education are as pencilled in by
the Department's planning branch. And because these assumptions may quite possibly turn out to be wrong may not your
report be in danger of being irrelevant before it is presented?
Or can you force the Government to attend to these questions
before it is too late?

There is one final omission from your terms of reference
which is perhaps the most important of all. You have not been
asked to inquire into the role of the Secretary of State for
Education and Science. This is significant and possibly sinister
because the Secretary of State's situation in teacher training is
quite different from what it is in other parts of education. Her
legal position is much more formidable, as we show in Chapter
7 of this book. This means that what is done elsewhere openly
by agreed circulars and published reports is done in teacher
training by administrative acts. An example of this is that,
while staff–student ratios in further education have been a
matter for a report by a committee, in colleges of education
they were fixed by a letter from the Department. This means
that it is the Secretary of State's responsibilities which are in the
most urgent need of scrutiny. This issue was dodged by the
Area Training Organization inquiry, and the House of Commons Select Committee inquiring into teacher training never
managed to find a way round the conventions of ministerial
omnipotence. But will not the work of your committee be
vacuous unless it investigates this crucial question of control
by the Secretary of State and the means by which this control
is exercised?

It may seem after all this that your condition is hopeless, but
despite the disadvantages you face, we do not believe that it
is. We hope our book will show you a way out. We hope your
committee will not waste its short life in documenting what is
wrong. That has been done already. Nor need it seek to refine
general recommendations for improvement. Your first task is
to propose ways and means. It will not be enough to suggest
change: we need to know in detail how change is to be
effected. Can you propose not only policy but the instruments

for its implementation? Only if you can will the inquiry which you have been asked to conduct be of any use or even of any interest. And it is to this end that the final section of our book relates. Many of our suggestions in this section are designed to make possible the curricular changes advocated earlier. For example, we believe that new associations between schools and colleges will require new relationships between different functional levels of teacher, qualification and salary. A rationally devised Burnham scale of salaries, linked to the Pelham scale, could be a powerful spur to the changes we propose. We suggest that redesigning the B.Ed. to serve professional ends requires new academic structures of which the Council for National Academic Awards offers the most promising example. What we have sought to do, in short, is to show the kind of means that would achieve the ends we desire. You may not agree with our proposals: you surely cannot ignore our approach.

Perhaps an example or two may help here. There seems to be a growing pressure from vice-chancellors and the Treasury among others to turn the colleges of education into liberal arts colleges to mop up the demand for higher education at a lower level than that of a university degree. Your terms of reference do not ask you to consider this. But the institutional approach will enable you to make recommendations about the form of administration and control which would be most conducive to the success of this policy were it to be adopted. You may come to recommend, for example, that if the future of the colleges of education lies in this direction, then they ought to be linked administratively as well as academically with universities. You can also seek to show what might be the consequences of such a policy, for the overall supply of teachers and for certain specialists.

Similarly, you may be urged to turn the colleges of education into multi-vocational colleges, training people for all kinds of social work. Your terms of reference could be said to encourage you to discuss this. Here again, your committee will achieve significance if it spells out the institutional consequences of such a policy. You might decide, for example, that such institutions should remain under the administration of

central and local government. You might consider the effect
of the size of existing institutions on such a proposal. You
might wonder how far the courses thus offered might have
aspects in common and, if so, whether the qualifications gained
could be interchangeable in terms of careers and salary structures later – and what precisely a multi-vocational college
means if this is not so.

Finally, you will have to face quite squarely the means by
which the schools are to be supplied with teachers in the light
of whatever recommendations you may make. Unless we can
be assured of that, we shall hardly be able to take you
seriously.

Above all, we would urge you to think of the present situation as neither static nor ordained. The schools must change,
in the interests of the children in them. The schools *can* change
if we reform the education and training of teachers. We believe
that if you can transcend the limitations of your establishment
and terms of reference you can still make this more likely.

All that remains for me now is to wish you and your colleagues a very happy year and to assure you that we are ready
to assist in any way that seems appropriate.

Yours sincerely
Tyrrell Burgess

Part One
The Students and the Colleges of Education

1 | Focus on the Student Teachers
Donald Lomax

Introduction

The purpose of this chapter is to say something about teachers in training and to evoke a picture of the kind of young people who seem destined to care for our children. To sharpen and deepen our picture, attention will be focused on a carefully selected and stratified random sample of students drawn from one college of education. There are sound reasons for believing that the young people the reader will meet within the following pages are usefully representative of many teachers in training, for in terms of intelligence, a wide range of personality factors, personal values, home background, school experience and scholastic achievement they are similar to students in other colleges of education.

The college

The college from which the student sample was drawn is situated on the boundary of a large industrial city and has more than 1400 men and women students in attendance. The attractive spacious grounds contain pleasant new teaching blocks and large halls of residence. In addition to the usual teaching accommodation the campus contains gymnasia, a sports hall, a swimming pool, a drama studio, assembly halls, art and design studios, an exhibition gallery and science laboratories. The college library holds over sixty thousand volumes and provides an excellent service of books and periodicals for reference and loan in all areas of college work. The students who have been selected to take advantage of these facilities are taught by a highly qualified staff of over 150 lecturers. Non-graduate students, aiming to obtain the teacher's certificate, study for three years a variety of subjects within the department of education, which provides courses in psychology, philosophy, sociology, history and the practice of education. In addition they study two further subjects which are chosen from courses offered by a relatively wide range of academic departments. Within the academic departments students may devote their time to American studies, art and design, drama, English, French, German, Russian, geography, history, music, religious studies, physical education, mathematics, biology, chemistry, physics and sociology. Students who are able to satisfy basic university entrance requirements may study to obtain the degree of Bachelor of Education. These students study a variety of subjects within the department of education for four years, one academic subject for four years, and a second academic subject for three years. A one-year postgraduate course leading to the university certificate in education is also provided for over a hundred students. The college is thus one of the largest in the country, having good facilities, a highly qualified staff, and a large student population following a relatively wide range of courses. It is possible that the majority of our teachers may be educated at colleges of this type in the future. The student teachers who are described in the following pages are in many ways successful young people. In order to see them in perspective we shall look firstly at their homes and schools before going on to consider their personal characteristics.

Homes and families

The young teachers in our sample faithfully reflect the national pattern of student recruitment in terms of social class. As a relatively small percentage of working-class children are successful in the selective school system it is not surprising that teachers should tend to come from middle-class groups. An analysis of the occupations of our students' fathers shows that approximately 30 per cent of them belong to professional or managerial groups, another 30 per cent belong to lower professional or clerical groups, whilst a further 30 per cent are classified in supervisory or skilled manual categories. The remaining 10 per cent of the fathers are either self-employed or work in semi-skilled jobs. Children of men belonging to the unskilled manual group are thus markedly absent from this student population. Like many other institutions, the college under discussion has consistently and unconsciously recruited its annual student intake according to this socio-economic pattern for some years past. It will, therefore, be obvious that the children of professional middle-class groups are strongly represented within the student body, whilst those of the semi-skilled or unskilled groups have seldom been able to avail themselves of this opportunity for further education.

Seventy per cent of the students considered that their homes were in middle-class areas and as might be expected their families lived in houses of good quality. Thirty-three per cent of the families lived in detached houses or bungalows; 46 per cent in semi-detached houses; 15 per cent in terraced houses which were sometimes of modern design; and 6 per cent in flats. Almost half the houses had adjoining garages and most of them had gardens. The families also enjoyed a relatively wide range of material possessions. Approximately 70 per cent of the families owned cars and such lesser luxuries as electric blankets, electric kettles and hairdriers, whilst almost all possessed television sets, radios, washing machines, vacuum cleaners, refrigerators and cookers. Many also owned record players, tape recorders, electric sewing machines, electric toasters and electric clocks. A smaller group of people possessed such articles as cine-cameras, projectors, dishwashers and knitting machines. Although many of the items listed above are not luxuries as measured by current standards it will be obvious that the students had enjoyed a relatively high level of material comfort. No student could be found who had any personal experience of slum conditions.

The parents belonged to a generation that had been deeply involved in fighting the last war in Europe and had survived to see their children accept some of the results of victory. Seventy per cent of the fathers and 10 per cent of the mothers had served in the armed forces. Over half the fathers had experienced service overseas in such areas as Europe, North Africa, South Africa, the Middle East, the Far East and the United States. By the time their children entered college parents on average had reached their early fifties, but there was a wide range of ages which resulted in a wide range of family circumstances. Just under half the parents had married before 1939 and a quarter during the war. Their families tended to be small with the average number of children being two. Half the students were in fact only or first-born children and a further 35 per cent were the second born in their families. Some students had younger brothers or sisters who were still at secondary or even primary school, while others had older brothers or sisters who were already established in jobs and were married with families of their own. In a majority of cases these older children had secured jobs of high status. The list of these jobs included, for example, an airline director, a veterinary surgeon, several types of professional engineers, a chartered accountant, a marketing director, a pharmacist, a surveyor, various civil servants, several physiotherapists, various teachers, bank officials, sales representatives and a store buyer. Only just over 10 per cent of the older siblings were employed in skilled manual jobs and none were employed in semi-skilled or unskilled occupations. Generally speaking it would seem that the factors which had helped the students in our sample to succeed had already made contributions towards the successes achieved by their older brothers and sisters. When the school experience of all the siblings, who were of secondary-school age or above, was analysed, it was found that approximately half of them attended grammar schools and that only a quarter attended secondary-modern schools. The remainder had been educated in private schools, technical schools or comprehensive schools.

Although many parents had been successful in their chosen careers, the group as a whole had limited experience of selective secondary schools and further education. Only a third of the parents had personal experience of grammar schools and only a sixth of them had continued their secondary education beyond the age of sixteen. However some 40 per cent of the fathers and 25 per cent of the mothers had received further education at technical college, teacher training college, secretarial college or university. Although only a quarter of the parents had obtained the School Certificate, virtually all the fathers who had continued to study had obtained further qualifications and made good progress in their careers. The picture for mothers was markedly different, for only half of the minority who sought further training had obtained extra qualifications and at the time their children entered college half of them were housewives and few held jobs of high status or responsibility. The kind of career success which many of the students' fathers had experienced had also been enjoyed by other relatives. Over half of the families had relatives who were teachers and over a third had relatives in other professions.

Both parents centred many of their interests on the home and devoted a considerable amount of time to television, radio, house decorating and gardening. There were of course different patterns of activity for men and women. Mothers often enjoyed cooking, knitting and sewing but had little time to spare for reading or watching sports. The sporting interests of fathers were also often fewer than the news coverage by mass media might suggest. A third of the fathers enjoyed association football and a sixth of them cricket, but tennis, rugby, golf, athletics and horse racing had only minority appeal. The only sport to appeal to mothers was lawn tennis and even in this case only one in eight of them expressed keen enjoyment. In general it seemed that both parents had little time for what have been traditionally described as cultural interests. Less than half of the fathers had any interest in reading and only a quarter enjoyed classical music. Less than a quarter of the mothers found time for occasional visits to the theatre and although a similar number still enjoyed dancing, their husbands had lost interest in this activity. Over 90 per cent of both sexes had no interest in such arts as opera, painting or ballet. Generally speaking there seemed to be little concern for either religion or politics and very few people were involved in any kind of social work. Three-quarters of the students' fathers did not hold strong political opinions and on the whole they seemed to find politics to be about as interesting as woodwork, finding the subject less appealing than football but more enjoyable than dancing. Taking mothers as a whole the level of political interest was the same as that shown in bingo or pottery, with only three in every hundred finding the subject important. At the 1966 general election 34 per cent of the fathers and 26 per cent of the mothers had voted for the Labour Party, while 53 per cent of the fathers and 54 per cent of the mothers had voted for the Conservative Party. The Liberal Party had attracted the votes of 1 per cent of the fathers and 7 per cent of the mothers. In almost 80 per cent of the families both parents voted for the same political party. A quarter of the mothers had an interest in religion, which meant that for the group as a whole the subject was more important than dancing but of less consequence than garden cultivation or dressmaking. One-tenth of the fathers concerned themselves with religion and an identical number were committed to car maintenance.

Most families took one daily newspaper and at least one of the Sunday papers. The *Daily Express* was the most favoured weekday reading, with the *Daily Mail*, *Daily Mirror* and the *Daily Telegraph* coming some way behind. The *Guardian*, *The Times* and the *Morning Star* only appealed to a small minority of families. On Sundays the *Sunday Express* was a firm favourite, but the 'quality' publications also had good sales with both the *Observer* and the *Sunday Times* being popular. Mothers tended to read the newspapers which fathers bought but supplemented their reading by taking a range of women's magazines, of which the most popular were *Woman* and *Woman's Own*. Fathers had less interest in magazines although small numbers enjoyed those which were concerned with motoring or gardening.

The one area in which the parents had invariably shown a high level of interest was their children's education. At the infant- and junior-school stages, mothers were the major family influence, but by the time that the secondary stage was reached fathers had usually assumed equal importance. No student had had a mother who took little interest in primary education and only a few reported that throughout their secondary-school careers their fathers had 'left it all to Mum'. Mothers usually had good contacts with both the infant and junior schools, feeling that they understood something of what the schools were trying to do and finding that it was possible to go to the school to discuss problems informally with the teachers. At the secondary stage, however, these contacts became much less frequent. On average parents had little contact with the secondary-school staff and became increasingly unable to offer advice to their children. Those mothers and fathers who were determined to do their best attended sports days, swimming galas, school plays and occasional meetings with the school staff, but others slowly lost contact with the system and relied entirely on their

offspring to give them relevant information. The adolescents
who found themselves in this position of power were able to
turn it to their own advantage. Although students, as a whole,
felt that their parents had given them moderately good educational guidance, this was an overgenerous verdict. It was, however, perhaps significant that no student could be found in the
group who had experienced any opposition to their educational
plans. The small number of parents who had been of some help
to their children had shown little positive interest but had not
hindered the educational process. Most students felt that their
parents had continued to maintain a high level of interest
throughout their college careers, although as the years passed
it had become increasingly difficult for many of the older folk
to understand a system that was frequently outside their own
experience.

Three-quarters of the students felt that they had had good
conditions for study at home and only 4 per cent believed that
home study conditions had been rather poor. In these cases
the problem was usually associated with either working in an
inadequately heated bedroom or with distracting noise from a
near-by television set. No student reported either very poor
home study conditions or any form of deliberate interference
by any other member of the family. The results of an objective
test, designed to explore recollected childhood feelings, indicated that during the early years at home not only had there
been a high degree of interaction between the student and the
parents but that this interaction had been mainly of a warm
and positive nature. Not surprisingly, perhaps, during the first
ten years of life there had been greater total interaction with
mother than with father. There had been an equally small
amount of negative or hostile interaction with both parents,
but a much greater degree of positive interaction with mother.
There had, of course, sometimes been difficulties during adolescence, but by the time students completed their college careers
they usually considered that their relationships with their
parents were good. When they looked back over their years in
school and college, students could neither recall any serious
shortage of material possessions nor any examples of parental
opposition to their studies.

Schools

The students had, generally speaking, been happy throughout their school careers. Even allowing for the fact that people remember selectively and often only consciously recall happy times, there was a marked absence from the student body of those gifted but troublesome people who find it hard to fit into school establishments. Our students tended to be people who knew the rules of the educational game and, by keeping to them, avoided serious clashes with authority. At the infant and junior schools it was usual for the students to have made good progress at their lessons. Some reported that their infant school had had two streams, but no one who had reached college had started in the second stream, nor could they recall any friends who had successfully transferred to the 'best class'. There were usually two streams at the junior school and again at this level virtually all our sample had been in the top stream. Some recalled children being transferred from a lower group into a higher, but few of these transferred children seemed to have been successful at the 11-plus examination. The names given to classes were sometimes evocative. One man reported that he had been a member of 'the top class', but had to pause to try and recall the name given to the lower stream. Eventually he said: 'I think we just called them "the others".' It seems to be members of 'the top class' who arrive at college; 'the others' go somewhere else. When they looked back on their primary-school experience most students felt that they had been moderately well taught, but few were enthusiastic about the experience. Half of the sample believed that most children at their primary schools came from working-class backgrounds, whilst 85 per cent believed that at the grammar-school stage the majority of their school-mates came from middle-class homes.

It will be seen from Table 1 that most students had obtained their secondary education in maintained grammar schools. The figures are similar to those produced by the Robbins Committee for their samples of students who were in colleges of education in 1962 and 1964. Of the present sample who were in colleges of education in 1968, over two-thirds had attended single-sex schools and had frequently found that this hindered the development of social skills.

Table 1 Type of Secondary School attended by Students

Type of secondary school	Percentage of students attending
Grammar	70
Secondary modern and grammar	4
Grammar and further education	3
Private and grammar	6
Private	4
Comprehensive	3
Technical college	4
Secondary modern	3
Secondary modern and further education	3
Total	100

Some 70 per cent of the students had been streamed on entry to their secondary school and most had been streamed at some stage. Many students had also had experience of 'setting' procedures in various subjects. In their internal organizational schemes most schools had used the traditional type of house system, but very few students felt that these arrangements had been a source of interest to either staff or pupils. As far as school academic study was concerned they felt that up to the fifth-form stage, schools considered homework to be moderately important. The stress on homework, however, greatly increased in the fifth form as the O-level examinations approached, and then reduced in the sixth form when the timetable was relaxed to allow pupils more freedom in planning their work. The average number of O-level passes was seven and the distribution of these passes suggested that most schools had adopted the traditional grammar-school curriculum. All the students had obtained the pass in English language as this was an essential qualification for college entrance, and half had been successful in English literature, French, mathematics, history and geography. One-third of the college intake had passssed in biology, one-fifth in religious knowledge and one-sixth in art. Smaller numbers had achieved passes in physics, chemistry, general science, German, Latin and Spanish. School staff had played a dominant role in planning the students' courses of study, for by this time parents knew too little about the system to be able to intervene confidently, and pupils could do little save accept staff decisions. Head teachers were usually vague, shadowy administrators seldom encountered outside morning assembly. When they were called upon to give advice, usually towards the end of the pupils' school career, they often had too little information upon which to act. Indeed in some cases their advice had been quite unhelpful. Relationships between staff and pupils naturally varied greatly, but the general, unenthusiastic verdict was that the staff as a whole had been only moderately pleasant people. At opposite extremes there were a few teachers who had almost ruined a pupil's academic career and others who in a masterly fashion had contrived to change for the better the whole course of a pupil's life. Generally speaking the students believed that the school staff had done a moderately good job in preparing them for the examinations. Two-thirds of the sample had received some training in examination techniques, and those who mastered these were to find them an invaluable aid to success for the rest of their school and college careers. Although pupils had taken only a moderate amount of interest in most of the subjects passed at O-level they had found much greater pleasure in their A-level studies and also gave much greater praise to the efforts of their teachers. Fifty-seven per cent of the students had gained two or more passes at this examination, with the highest levels of performance being achieved in such arts subjects as English, geography and history. Far fewer students had gained passes in the sciences. The pass rate may have been influenced by some unfortunate cases of pupils not being allowed to study their most favoured subjects because of difficulties connected with either school timetables or staffing problems. In these circumstances pupils felt that they must bow inevitably to the superior wisdom of the school. Unfortunately careers guidance was also often poor, and 30 per cent of the students had attended schools which did not have a careers teacher. Even in schools which did have a teacher specially appointed to give careers advice, there were some odd situations. 'At our school,' said one young woman, 'careers guidance was a cupboard!' The cupboard in question contained varied literature which was intended to serve as guidance for the young people who were trying to plan their lives. It had obviously been difficult for many young people to plan their careers in the absence of the relevant information. The comfortable conveyor belt on which they sat carried them to universities or colleges and to get off meant taking a leap into the unknown. Only 20 per cent of the students had had the ambition to gain university entrance at the sixth-form stage and many had drifted uncertainly. Eventually half of the sample arrived at college as a result of a process of complete drift. Some told bizarre tales. One handsome young man had arranged to join his father in attending to the needs of a motorcar show-room. By chance he visited an old friend at college and over a few drinks in the bar listened to colourful descriptions of the possibilities of college social life. After a few more drinks he became convinced that 'It would be a bit of a laugh to let Dad manage the showrooms himself for a year and live it up for a bit . . . so I came and it was a hell of a first term!' He narrowly escaped expulsion twice in the first year, became seriously in-terested in physical education in the second, grew fiercely critical of people who had the wrong professional attitude in the third, gained distinctions in his final examinations, and then went to the United States where he successfully obtained a degree. Only a quarter of the students seemed to have entirely avoided the process of drift and to have planned their careers. Taking the sample as a whole, understanding of both the advan-tage and disadvantage of a career in teaching seemed to be very limited. This was perhaps not surprising in view of the absence of help in planning for the years to follow school. Parents were full of good intentions. 'They said they just wanted me to be happy.' 'My mother wanted me to get the best I could out of life.' 'Daddy was pleased that I wanted to do something else.' This helpful general support was not, however, an adequate substitute for specific careers guidance. If the young pupils had additional personal problems at this stage, things were even more difficult, for whilst almost 70 per cent of the schools had a member of staff ostensibly taking responsibility for careers, under 3 per cent had a teacher specifically responsible for pastoral care or counselling. It seemed, therefore, that some schools had not been able to prepare students adequately for their college experience. In fact some 86 per cent of the students had not received any kind of specific pre-college instruction and over 60 per cent had not even been instructed in the use of libraries.

Students

The obvious things which are quickly apparent to those who know students are that they are usually pleasant, healthy and attractive people. They are also able. When we consider the performance of our present sample of young teachers on a test of high-grade intelligence, we find that the top 10 per cent of them compare favourably, in terms of test scores, with the most able groups of university students. In addition, we see that approximately half of the college group obtain test scores close to the average score attained by university students. A more detailed analysis, provided by individual intelligence tests, shows the students to have particularly high levels of verbal ability. It therefore seems unlikely that, generally speaking, there is a shortage of intellectual power in colleges. As we have already seen, this ability has been used to cope with the demands of the school system and to achieve examination results which often meet the basic requirements for university entrance. It seems that the more likely danger in this situation is that student ability might be underestimated. In some cases there does not seem to be any clear knowledge of the ability levels which are necessary to achieve success on certain college courses and sometimes the required levels are lower than the course teachers would expect. An interesting example was provided by the charming young lady whose intelligence scores were well below those of any other student. Towards the close of her college career she was asked about her interest in various studies. She had only 'moderate interest' in her main academic subjects.

Well there was nothing else I could do except creative embroidery, but you are not given enough freedom. I'd rather do as I want, getting just a little bit of influence from other people ... but I think we were influenced too much. You know, we were told what to do and everything ... I don't like it!

If the young lady's interest in art was rather limited it was even lower in her subsidiary academic courses.

Well, I was quite interested in biology at school, but I'm afraid they killed it when I came to college ... no interest, no, none.

No I've never been interested in history, not even at school ... but I couldn't see what else to do.

Her studies in education had also made little impact.

Philosophy? I hardly know what it is. It's an awful thing to admit I know ... but I just don't understand it. ... I've no interest.

Well, I just sit there in psychology lectures and it just goes over my head. I don't know what anybody is talking about at all . . . no interest.

And so the story went on through one subject after another until at last she gave her general verdict on the whole experience.

Well I think the courses could have been made a lot more interesting. I think a lot of it is due to the fact that some of the lecturers talk over everybody's head. Some of the lecturers aren't very good. They think people understand them but they don't. ... Quite frankly I've had a very boring time.

The student teacher went on to say that there were no social questions causing her concern. As for the Christian Church, she said, 'I tend to think that it will fade away. The Church isn't important to me, not really.' She sought no political changes? 'No not really ... because I don't know enough about it.' In the education system she wanted 'more schools'. Did this mean more comprehensive schools?

Well I don't know. ... I haven't thought about it. Yes! I think it is better to have all different ranges of ability together rather than all the clever ones in one school and all the thickies in another.

On teaching practice the student did well and her final examination results were quite satisfactory. Although this young teacher lacked interest in her studies and knew little of the society she lived in, she was industrious. The attitude towards work which had enabled her to achieve, over the years, a collection of seven passes at O-level, was sufficient to get her through her college course. She had seemingly had the good fortune to choose courses which demanded little more than average general intelligence. In other areas of college studies, rigorous intellectual demands, similar to those experienced by university undergraduates, were made upon the students. Some were angry about the different levels of difficulty discovered in different courses. One man claimed that it was his major grievance.

I am really annoyed about the discrepancy between various syllabuses in departments. I could have had a really easy time, but I picked a tough department and I've had to work like hell!

In the research project upon which this chapter is based, the scores on a battery of group and individual intelligence tests were studied in relation to eleven different college criteria of successful student performance. The analysis revealed that different patterns of ability were associated with different criteria of successful performance at college. Whilst this kind of finding may not seem in itself remarkable, it may serve to indicate how little is known about student abilities, for in most colleges it seems likely that staff would assume the relationship between ability and performance to be a much simpler problem. It seems possible that further studies of student abilities and performance might help us to refine further our selection procedures.

The results of an extensive psychological test battery suggested that the students in the sample under discussion were not only very able people but were also, on average, well-balanced personalities. They seemed to enjoy good health in both physical and mental terms. Whilst average personality profiles for the sexes tend to conceal a wide range of individual differences, it seemed that there were enough personality differences between the sexes to suggest that further research might prove to be fruitful. Generally speaking, male students tended to be more aggressive and also more self-controlled, while women students tended to be more sensitive, more introverted and more excitable. Men strove harder for success through personal effort, were more likely to withdraw after failure, were more likely to have dreams of public recognition, and were more intellectual. Women tended to be more restrained, more interested in excitement and in aesthetic experiences.

Further evidence of differences between the sexes was provided by a test of motivational structures. Men it seemed had stronger destructive hostile impulses at both the conscious and unconscious levels. They also had a stronger conscious drive towards self-assertion and achievement. Women also made stronger emotional attachments. Another test, this time of motivational patterns revealed in the teaching situation, found men to be more inadequate than women in adult roles, often gaining pleasure by vicariously participating in the activities of their pupils. Men were also significantly more concerned with obtaining reassurances of their superiority and value, often justifying their dominant attitude in the classroom situation by stressing the need to maintain discipline. Women students were more warm and loving in their relationships with children, and justified their attitude on the grounds that a child's greatest need is love. They were also significantly more non-directive in their approach to children than were men. They stressed the integrity of the child, and sought to minimize the child's expression of dependency. A study of the differences between the sexes in personal values showed the men to be more intersted in economic and political values, whilst the women placed more stress on the aesthetic. This study of differences between the sexes is only one example of the kind of interesting, and possibly useful, findings which emerge from the study of college group differences. It seems very likely at the present time that colleges know too little about group differences and, therefore, are unable to give them the attention which they may merit. Some group differences are, of course, obvious. If we return to our previous example – the differences between men and women students – we find that there are some which are strikingly clear. It is, for example, usually the men who dominate the organization of clubs and societies. As a result they tend to enjoy a better social life within the college. Women students are often remarkable for their passivity and apathy. An example taken from the particular college under discussion may serve to illustrate the point. On one occasion the women students had arranged a table-tennis match against women from another college, but unfortunately one of the team of three was unwell and a replacement was sought. From a college population of a thousand women one would expect that at least one reserve table-tennis player would emerge. No player could be found. In desperation the two fit players searched for any woman who would simply hold a bat so that the match could go on. No woman student could be found to perform this task and at a late hour the match was cancelled. It is only fair to point out that women students seldom showed this degree of apathy in their studies. There were, however, some worrying problems connected with the levels of student interest in their studies, and it is to these problems that we next turn.

On the whole, students were interested in their main academic subject but only moderately interested in their subsidiary academic studies. Attitudes to the basic curriculum courses were, however, even less enthusiastic. There was only moderate interest in the English course, very slight interest in mathematics, and hardly any interest in either physical education or religious knowledge. When students were asked to put their own feelings aside and say how important they thought these courses were, they said that they were all moderately important except physical education, which they considered to be rather unimportant. Some savage things were said not only about course content, but also about the performance of lecturers teaching these courses. One man simply gave a bitter laugh when asked to rate the importance of one curriculum course, then after a long intake of breath he commented: 'When I think of all those wasted flaming hours spent listening to that stuff! Irrelevant things mostly. . . . I don't think even the lecturers knew what it was about . . . some of them were more bored than I was . . . and then they come out and criticize you on teaching practice!'

Attitudes to the numerous courses offered within the department of education varied considerably. Psychology was generally thought to be interesting, and there was moderate interest in sociology. There was, however, only slight interest in the history of education and virtually no interest whatsoever in philosophy. If one takes the view that an understanding of the philosophical basis of educational thought should underpin all other studies then prospects were indeed poor. Students considered the subject to be 'dull'; 'irrelevant'; utterly confusing'; 'over our heads'; 'a real bore'; and 'a waste of everybody's time'. Some members of staff reacted by saying that the subject was unsuitable for this age group; others felt that the students were of such low intellectual ability that it was impossible to teach them.

The reader who is unfamiliar with the workings of colleges may by now be wondering how students can possibly fit so much into a three-year course. Is it possible to study a main academic subject, a subsidiary academic subject, curriculum courses such as English, mathematics, physical education and religious knowledge, in addition to a range of subjects in education which includes philosophy, psychology, sociology and the history of education, not to mention weekly courses in educational practice and the courses now offered in such things as comparative education, visual aids and curriculum development? The answer might be that it is possible to do all these things, just so long as we do not expect them all to be done well. At the present time students seem to be studying many things which do not interest them. Someone, somewhere must believe that this, in the end, will be good for them. When the students considered the whole curriculum, their general verdict was that they were only moderately interested. As research was not usually done on student attitudes within the college, most members of staff were unaware of this situation.

The general student verdict on the staff as a whole was that they were only moderately interesting people. Lecturers in the academic subjects were often found to be interesting, but not when they were teaching curriculum courses. On these occasions they became 'rather uninspiring'. In the department of education lecturers in psychology and sociology were usually found to be interesting, but lecturers in the history of education were found to be uninspiring and those in philosophy were described as being 'very dull'. Only one-fifth of the students described the whole college staff as interesting people, and not even one student would go so far as to describe the entire staff as 'very stimulating'. One-tenth of the students – a sizeable minority group – dismissed the whole staff as a 'rather uninspiring' group of people.

Faced by much in their studies that seemed to be irrelevant to their career prospects, the young teachers approached teaching practice with added enthusiasm. Even though the experience in schools had sometimes been difficult, students as a whole rated it as very valuable. Though it was not unknown for some to find periods of practice 'irksome', 'ill-planned' and 'badly directed', it seemed that this work was at least relevant to the job waiting to be done in the real world. No other area of college work was considered to be of equal value. Perhaps in an ideal college course, teaching practice would be one of a number of equally exciting experiences, but with courses being what they were, the few weeks spent in the town primary school were still vividly recalled when a hundred lectures had been lost beyond all recall. It may be that in reacting against the sheer bulk of their courses, students were greatly overestimating the value of teaching practice. They were, however, unenthusiastic about the professional training which they had received at college and considered it to be only moderately satisfactory.

Students found the discipline maintained by both the department of education and the academic departments to be only moderately strict, while discipline in the college as a whole was acknowledged to be rather lax. The official policy was to 'encourage the fullest academic and social freedoms of students compatible with their efficiency as students'. The young teachers thus found that these were happy years. On the whole they considered social life within the college to be moderately good, although women students were less enthusiastic than were the men. For most people these were happy times because the facilities of the area were excellent in many ways. It was, therefore, possible for some young people to have a very enjoyable time whilst completely ignoring college activities. Some women students stopped attending college social functions before the end of their first term and thereafter found their pleasures elsewhere.

An analysis of students' leisure, sporting and intellectual

interests showed that they devoted most of their energy to leisure activites, and that few gave time to the things which traditionally have been regarded as culturally important. Classical music, the theatre, art and literature were things which usually did not touch their lives. It seemed that poor reading habits had developed during school days and had persisted throughout the college years. The usual explanation offered was that students spent so many hours each week listening to lecturers' talk that they had time only to read their set books. Certainly few read anything else. Many did not even regularly read newspapers. When all their interests were considered it was hard to escape the conclusion that they were of a very limited range.

The amount of staff–student contact time has been traditionally large in colleges. It was not unusual to find that students spent twenty or more hours each week listening to lecturers talking whilst relatively little time was devoted to individual tutorial work. Outside the lecture situation students were moderately industrious, working on average eight hours per week. It would not be unfair however to describe a third of the students as either 'rather lazy' or 'very lazy', and approximately an eighth of the group coped with official college requirements by working for only one or two hours per week. Generally speaking students were satisfied with their choice of career and considered that their future prospects in teaching were quite good. However the paucity of career information, which was so apparent at the secondary-school stage, still persisted in the college. Many of the young teachers had little knowledge of the structure of their chosen profession, and virtually no knowledge of other career opportunities. The minority, who were aware of the disadvantages facing the non-graduate teacher, were less sanguine than the blissfully ignorant. Some women were particularly vague about their future work, and estimates of the teaching salary were as low as £400 a year. Other women had a vague notion that 'you are taxed and there are some other things they can take out of your pay'. It was not unusual to find a woman student with little interest in equal pay. On several occasions the point was strongly made by women, that 'men should get more because they are the main breadwinner ... what the wife earns is a sort of extra'. Material values did, however, merit some consideration and 60 per cent of the students felt that money was 'important'.

At the sixth-form stage only 20 per cent of our sample had had the ambition to gain entrance to a university. By the time that their college careers drew to a close, however, some 40 per cent of the students regretted not going to a university. Thus a large percentage of the college group had reached the conclusion that, for various reasons, the education they had received was second best. Less than 25 per cent of the group said that they intended to stay in teaching for more than twenty years. Some 2 per cent admitted that they intended to teach for less than two years and as many as 20 per cent could not guarantee to teach for more than five years. It seemed that the profession would soon lose many of those who had been so expensively trained. However, so few students had career plans and so few had any knowledge of other jobs that it seemed very likely that the process of drift, which had carried them to the college, would probably carry them back into the schools and perhaps leave them there becalmed.

An investigation into the social awareness of the student teachers produced some disquieting results. Questions were asked about the British way of life, the Christian Church, the educational system, social problems and political problems. Generalizing over the whole of their experience, a third of the students felt that life in modern Britain was barely tolerable, and a further 14 per cent went so far as to say that life was now unsatisfactory. The half of the student group who were happy with the conditions of modern life felt that this country was still a very desirable place in which to live. Those who were pessimistic seemed to have taken the loss of our 'former glories' to heart. 'It stands to reason,' said a blunt Northerner, 'we used to rule the lot . . . now you get them coming here telling us what to do. This National Debt . . . impossible to pay that back . . . we're an old country . . . bound to be tired.' A gifted man who had written over two hundred poems during his college career was worried by 'the laziness of people, the general indolence . . . too many people blaming the people at the top . . . probably feeling that they have no power to do anything themselves'. Another man took up a similar theme.

I very strongly believe that we should shorten the working week . . .
we could still get more production out. I'm sure we could have a
three-and-a-half day working week. Then there would be more
leisure and we would need to be educated to use it. . . . I have done
a few jobs but I have never worked a full day in my life yet – the
nearest I came to it was bus conducting and I got paid least if all for
that . . . which is typical really, isn't it?

Very few students had any interest in religion. Although they
dismissed the Christian Churches as largely irrelevant, most
students had little religious knowledge on which to base this
judgement. The results of an objective test of values threw
further light on this situation. The test provided a measure of
the relative importance of six basic interests and the results
showed that social values were most important to the students.
They were interested in people and tended to be kind, unselfish
and sympathetic. Their approach to life tended to be empirical,
critical and rational. Considerable importance was also given
to purely practical matters, although aesthetic experiences were
often more highly valued by women. At the bottom of the list
of values came the political and the religious. It seemed that
the students were neither interested in power nor in mystical
experience. Views on the Established Church tended to be scath-
ing: 'I think that religion is definitely on the downward trend
. . . on the way out.' This sentiment was frequently repeated:
'What part has the Church to play? None whatsoever!' One
man sounded a more optimistic note: 'I think the Church does
have a role in modern society, if it is completely radical. It must
allow itself to be crucified. I think the teachings of Christ have
had a tremendous influence over the last two thousand years . . .
it has altered the course of Western history. I have no interest
at all in the Church as an organization but if it helps to per-
petuate the ideas of Christ I'm all for it.' Many students however felt that the Church was 'completely finished' and was
irrelevant in modern Britain: 'I can't see any point in it really,
in many cases it's just a gathering of the well-off types. You find
that folk who have an important part to play at the church
regard themselves as being a cut above the others.' Only 7 per
cent of the students were regular church attenders, and half the
sample either attended very rarely or not at all. Fifty-five per

cent of the group, however, described themselves as Christian, some 17 per cent were agnostics and a similar number had not decided what they were. Only 6 per cent of the students claimed to be atheists.

The political opinions of the group were extremely naïve. Many women students said that they had no political views of any kind, although a few did want specific changes: 'I think the trade unions have too firm a hold. I suppose they have a use in some fields, but they tend to be that little bit too strong.' Others had a general feeling of unease: 'I am not satisfied at the moment with the situation. It seems that all the parties are getting to be the same. The Liberal Party is ineffective . . . so are the Conservatives . . . and the Labour Party has let me down. I'd still support them though, because basically they are the people with the ideals.' Some students dismissed politicians completely: 'I think politics is all self-gain'; 'You see, they tell so many silly stories that nobody listens to them now'; 'I hate the thought that so much that is said is untrue . . . propaganda . . . but what can you do? Anyway I don't really feel strongly; personal relationships are what matter to me.' Solutions to the vaguely perceived political problems were often equally vague: 'Well it's no good at the moment is it? I mean they do have the brain power to do something about putting the country right but instead they are continually pulling against one another . . . fighting . . . it won't get them anywhere. I'd like to see them all pulling together not against each other!' Some women could go no further than advocating very brief general solutions to rational problems: 'I'd like it all sorted out!'; 'We need more effective parties'; 'They do too much talking'; 'More people helping the country to get back on its feet'. Others wanted the world to be generally a better place: 'I would like to see more equality. I think communism is a good idea in principle, but I don't see how it can work . . . I don't think it will ever happen . . . it's never going to be perfect is it? Materialism is at the basis of the whole thing . . . self-seeking and selfishness. If people were less selfish there would be fewer problems.' One solution to the perceived problems, which was suggested by several students, was put typically by a sensitive man: 'I would like to see a coalition of the parties, where everybody joins together.

I am sure that this could take us above party politics. We need to make people aware ... make them think. I can't see it happening though ... too many people are out for number one.' It was clear from the many views that were expressed that students, as a whole, felt that things were not going well for the country. There was a lack of understanding of politics and government which was coupled with a cynical attitude towards politicians.

Social problems did not worry all students, but the colour problem caused many some concern: 'Well, on the immigration question I think they've got to be thick skinned, these coloured people. If I was coloured and came to this country, I'd either bump myself off or go back on the next boat. I couldn't stand these jokes.' Another man took a harder line:

I would very much like Britain to stick as it is now ... stop this immigration now before it gets worse ... get the damned problem sorted out ... educate what we've got already here but make this the limit. I mean, to put it quite bluntly and accurately, we have got a lot of uneducated wogs in the place. I'm not colour conscious at all ... the truth is I have nothing against them as people – I know some intelligent ones who I am good friends with ... but half of them don't know what they are doing here!

There was also some general unease over problems which were currently topical: 'Well, there's the problem of traffic and then there's slum clearance ... but I can't think of any way of improving it, but something needs to be done'; 'Capital punishment, that is important, it annoys me to hear people wanting it back. I get very annoyed when I hear people saying that prisoners are treated too well. The chap might be inside for thirty years ... who is going to begrudge him a radio?'; 'I don't approve of prescription charges and I think there's too much talk about people using the system ... these people are in a minority. Most working blokes feel degraded if they don't have a job. I know my father does if he hasn't got a job. I think people get carried away when they see that the line at the labour exchange is a mile long.'

Some students thought that things were 'all right': No, I don't think there are any particular social problems. This sort of thing enters my head for a time, and I think about it for an

hour or two and then it's gone again and I forget all about it';
'Oh! I think there's too much talk about social problems. People
should be pleased they can live in this country. When I think
of those lads I taught down in the city . . . you know all this talk
about home conditions . . . I honestly think it's a waste of time
having them in school, they'd be far better off out at work';
'Well perhaps there are one or two things to be done . . . I don't
know . . . I think that most people have enough. There was
something on television one night about how so many people
now have cars and very soon we'll have more cars than people.
Things are going pretty well really'; 'Yes, the only thing I would
point out is that the workers now have more money than the
middle class. The trouble is they don't save it. I believe there
is a lot of drinking and gambling. Then of course so many want
this national assistance as well!'

There was a wide variety of views on the necessary changes
to be made in the educational system, and there was some impatience: 'I want education more down to earth! Some educationalists get funny ideas! Let them call a spade a spade!'; 'I
think they should keep politics out of education. I don't agree
with comprehensives. Generally grammar-school children are
grammar-school material'; 'Public schools? I agree with them.
Let's face it, all animals were born equal but some are more
equal than others, and that still applies. There are superior
people just as there are superior cars on the road. You can't
run a superior car on inferior petrol'; 'I'd definitely like to see
more comprehensives brought in. I think it is important if only
for the coeducation. Single-sex schools don't fit you for the
adult world do they?'; 'I've mixed feelings about raising the
school-leaving age. There are so many people who are inedu-
cable. I thought, surely everybody must have some mission in
life . . . but there are so many jobs. So I have mixed feelings.
It could so easily be boredom for them and absolute hell for the
teacher!'; 'I don't think I will get involved in education because
I don't think I will be all that dedicated . . . frankly I can't see
any changes I want to make in education'; 'I think the big fault
with education is that it is so traditionally based and so slow
in changing. The educationalists and the psychologists are so far
ahead of the actual practical teaching. There is basically a lack

of communication between the two groups'; 'Well I think there are unrealistic attitudes ... you know trying to make the secondary-modern schools into copies or modified versions of the grammar schools'; 'Any changes in the educational system? Oh! gosh! I've never thought about this before! There probably are changes that we needed, but I haven't had any pointed out to me!'; 'Well, I don't really know enough about the system to suggest any changes, but I think I'd like to see external examiners to check on teachers ... because I think it's criminal what teachers sometimes get away with!'

Some problems

Although the scope of this chapter has been restricted by the limited space available, an attempt has been made to evoke a useful picture of student teachers by briefly describing, in non-technical terms, some of their characteristics. The young people described above seem to be usefully representative of many student teachers at present studying in large colleges of education.

Although the students have used their abilities to cope with the demands of the school system, many of them have lacked a sense of direction in the planning of their careers. If the schools are at fault, so are many colleges, for little informed careers advice is available at any time. It may be well argued that neither schools nor colleges should be asked to take this additional responsibility with their present resources. If this argument is accepted we must ask who else is to play the major role in vocational guidance? Although our students have obtained the necessary paper qualifications, they have virtually no interest in aspects of our culture which have been traditionally considered valuable, and they read few newspapers and fewer books. Their understanding of society and its problems may also seem to be very limited, and one is prompted to ask whether young teachers should not have greater social awareness? The colleges may have to shoulder some of the blame, for if the students are right, too much that is taught within their walls is irrelevant to the needs of the young teacher.

Further reading

B. J. Biddle and W. J. Elena (eds.), *Contemporary Research on Teacher Effectiveness*, Holt, Rinehart & Winston, 1964.

J. S. Bruner, *Towards a Theory of Instruction*, Harvard University Press, 1966.

B. S. Cane, *Research into Teacher Education*, National Foundation for Educational Research, 1968.

N. Gage (ed.), *Handbook of Research on Teaching*, Rand McNally, 1963.

L. Hudson, *Contrary Imaginations*, Penguin, 1967.

B. Jackson and D. Marsden, *Education and the Working Class*, Routledge & Kegan Paul, 1962; Penguin, 1966.

A. Morrison and D. McIntyre, *Teachers and Teaching*, Penguin, 1969.

W. Taylor, *Society and the Education of Teachers*, Faber, 1969.

S. Wiseman, *Education and Environment*, Manchester University Press, 1964.

2 The Student View
Peter Robinson

Few people able or prepared to promote change in the colleges of education have ever taken seriously the continuous criticism that successive generations of students have voiced about the nature of their courses, and their own role within the college community.

The Teacher's Certificate, which all students in colleges of education receive on the successful completion of their courses, is not a 'negotiable' qualification like so many others gained as a result of higher education. The Certificate qualifies its holders only for teaching, and consequently many students feel trapped into becoming part of what has already been described as a 'captive profession'[1]. Other college-of-education students criticize the low status they are accorded in comparison with students in universities and other sectors of higher education. Many more are concerned about the highly regulated nature of their institutions and, where they still exist, the single-sex colleges. There is a strong belief amongst students that the colleges should change their present 'mono-technic' character in favour of a more 'multipurpose' one. They claim to feel socially and educationally isolated, and seriously question whether this is the best environment in which to educate tomorrow's teachers[2]. Frequently the colleges fail to meet the basic professional and academic needs of their students, and similarly fail to understand their personal aspirations. In 1964, Peter Marris wrote:

While the growth of higher education has prompted a re-examination of its aims, the aims of its students remain unconsidered . . . the pattern of higher education cannot be decided only by the aspirations of its institutions. It must also take into account the needs which students will recognize as personally relevant[3].

This view holds particular significance for the work of the colleges of education – which until recently have been concerned primarily with meeting the expansionary calls of governments, and satisfying their own peculiar institutional aspirations. As a result, many courses have developed in a very piecemeal manner with little fundamental restructuring to take account of the personal needs of the modern student teacher. In 1960, when the three-year course of training was introduced, many educationalists hoped for a complete reassessment of the underlying philosophy on which the work of the colleges of education was based. Unfortunately this was not to be so, and today many students still complain about the length and irrelevance of their courses. It is amazing that many students still feel this way when the major professional association of teachers is already claiming that 'the demands that will be made upon teachers in the remaining decades of this century will necessitate the lengthening of the concurrent course to four years'[4].

It is the nature of the college course that has produced the severest criticism from students. The course itself, which is detailed in chapter 4, has four main parts: main subject studies, curriculum studies, education studies and practical teaching experience, and while there have been improvements in all these parts in most colleges since the introduction of the three-year course, there are still several serious criticisms. The greatest of these has centred around that part of the course related to the preparation of students for the classroom – their professional training. Most of the surveys undertaken to assess student attitudes to the professional elements of the course showed a very high degree of concern with the education course itself. Taken by all, and essential to all, it receives prime consideration from college of education students. At one particular college, 75 per cent of the students felt that they received insufficient professional training[5]. Other students surveyed claimed that 'the course places insufficient emphasis on the fact that you are training to teach'[6]. Similarly another complaint is that 'general teaching method' is given too little time in most courses. Education, as taught, is felt to have little relevance to the classroom. Many students wish to see greater emphasis on the teaching of reading, classroom organization, discipline problems and the teaching of immigrant children. Some students would like to see their education lectures and seminars more directly geared to practice.

Teaching practice itself is a highly valued part of professional training, but it has given rise to criticism and controversy for some years. Research into teaching practice has been dominated mainly by a desire to find an effective means of assessing students. However, a number of studies show not only that students consider this to be the most important part of their professional training, but that most of them would like to spend more time in schools[7]. (On average they spend between twelve to fifteen weeks on school practice during a three-year course.) Many students also feel that the best use is not being made of the present teaching practice periods. Criticism ranges from being expected to do too much written work during the practice – and as a result reducing the value of the practice itself – to lack of constructive help and criticism from supervisors. Shipman found that students viewed their college tutors as examiners rather than guides, and as a result the influence of the tutor was much less effective than it should have been[8]. In another study Sorensen found that a good deal of anxiety and hostility was generated by disagreements between students and supervisors about appropriate classroom behaviour[9]. These studies point out the difficulties faced by both tutors and students when planning and discussing teaching practice. The pressures on a student teacher at such times are considerable. He is trying to adapt to the demands made by his college supervisor, his class teacher, the children he is teaching – and also himself. As Shipman suggests:

Students have not only to adjust to individual teachers but to a school culture not synchronized with that of college. The consequent tension was resolved by students using two levels of professional value, one for use in college and one for use in the classroom, eventually resulting in the transitory influence of the college[10].

Students are critical that many of their teaching practice supervisors have little or no relevant teaching experience for the age group they are supervising. Many complain that college supervision is inadequate, and that they receive more useful help and criticism from teachers in the schools.

There are serious problems here, and the planning and supervision of teaching practice needs to be carefully considered and controlled. Indeed, one of the main arguments in favour of professional training before full-time teaching, rather than after, is that early experiences of teaching in the classroom are particularly formative, and should, therefore, be specially planned. As E. A. Allen points out: 'Generally the learning of the job can be made easier, more adventurous, more thorough and rapid, and given more momentum, if initial experiences are arranged and supervised with unobstrusive care'[11].

The scope and content of the education course is consistently questioned. A greater emphasis on the sociology and psychology of education is consistently called for[12] – the students favouring a psychological approach to education that concentrates on the practical rather than the academic.

Curriculum studies come in for serious criticism because in many ways they are 'merely a hotch-potch of subjects studied to a very low level with no rational justification, no stated aims or objectives and certainly no attempt to relate their relevance to main subject or education studies'[13].

The standard and content of main subject courses also cause much cynicism and dissatisfaction. Generally students seem quite satisfied with the amount of time they spend on main subject studies[14], although an appreciable number consistently claim that the standards of these courses are too low. At one college of education surveyed[15], the students made the following comments about the academic standard of their courses:

Not nearly enough emphasis is given to high-level academic achievement. Students need to be pushed and given a challenge to achieve something.

It seems difficult to combat the idea that because teachers are needed the college will 'get people through' the examinations.

More integration with the university on the academic as well as the social side would be useful with the aim of a college of education being a faculty of the university, so raising its status. It is most unfortunate that students here feel a certain inferiority which is completely unfounded.

The National Union of Students in its *Memorandum to the Robbins Committee* summed it up like this:

Amongst training college students the rate of wastage is very low. (This is still true today.) It is widely considered – even amongst the students themselves – that the rate of wastage is so low that it calls the standard and contents of the courses, and the value of the qualification gained, into question – and it may be that the national demand for teachers has had too great an effect on the standard of the course given [16].

The criteria employed in assessing students vary considerably from college to college and it is impossible to determine any consistency throughout the country. 'In the case of many colleges, assessment ranges from the idiosyncratic to the frankly eccentric' [17]. There is clearly a need for some coherent method of assessment to be developed.

Some studies have revealed that there is, predictably, a split between primary and secondary student teachers in their attitudes to main course studies; the former placing greater value on general curriculum subjects, the latter on study in 'greater depth' of one academic subject [18]. Some feel the colleges should, perhaps, differentiate their courses, and so provide study especially geared to the kind of school in which the student intends to eventually teach (infant, primary or secondary). Others claim, however, that it is in their best interests if every part of the course, no matter what its form, is as intellectually rigorous as any other. That a student happens to be training to be an infant- or junior-school teacher does not imply a less challenging education.

With the present concurrent form of training most students believe that a system of continuous assessment is fair and just. In the main, this is because success in college examinations has been shown to have little value in predicting the competence of a teacher, and as Taylor points out:

The fact that the final grades obtained in both theory and practice play virtually no part in helping or hindering the student to obtain first appointments, are never taken into account subsequently, and have been shown to have no significant correlation with later promotion and teaching success, reinforces the impression that the final examinations have a purely nominal function as far as the maintenance of standards and the predictive ranking of teacher competence is concerned [19].

A fairly drastic overhaul of the present balance of teaching within their courses is frequently demanded by students. In all recent surveys, from Robbins to the latest authoritative report from the National Union of Students' 'Commission on Teaching in Higher Education' (1969), the majority of students feel that too little time is spent in tutorials and seminars, and too much reliance placed on lectures. In the NUS survey, at one of the two colleges of education surveyed, an average of 15.4 hours per week was spent on formal lectures, and only 3.5 hours per week on seminars and tutorials [20]. The students of the colleges of education were the most 'intensively lectured' group in higher education, and they themselves clearly felt substantially over-lectured. An indictment of the lecture was that 60 per cent of the NUS sample had 'neutral or worse' feelings about its effectiveness as a method of teaching. The students in the colleges express the common criticisms of the lecture method and of lectures: 'ill-prepared', 'mumbles', little opportunity to ask questions', 'spoon-feeding', 'badly presented'. These comments on the ineffectiveness of this type of teaching are confirmed by John McLeish's researches into the 'lecture method':

Students listening to an uninterrupted discourse within their range of understanding and taking notes in their normal fashion carry away something of the order of 40 per cent of the factual data, the theoretical principles stated and the general applications referred to by the lecturer. A week later they have forgotten at least half of this material. But there are considerable individual differences of the order of 3 : 1 between the best and worst cases [21].

Even accepting that in some colleges the lecturer rather than the lecture method may be at fault, most students would like the number of compulsory lectures reduced, and the time for various types of discussion increased.

The students in one college of education found it ironic that a lecturer in education and teaching method should himself be incapable of communicating effectively. 'Lecturers don't even practice what they preach,' said one, citing a lecturer who taught for an hour and a half on the theme that lessons of more than fifty minutes have been shown to be inefficient. At the same college a lecturer insisted on the unreliability of essay-type examinations, then in the sessional examinations asked her students to write an essay on this very point. Lecturers, the students complained, taught ideas they didn't live up to. Examination cramming was condemned for schools but practised in colleges. The popular theory of individualized and child-orientated learning, advocated for the children in the schools, was never applied to the colleges themselves. 'Do as I say, not as I do.' It was felt that the staff were either inexperienced or out of touch with students and modern schooling[22].

Because of the students' commitment (in many cases compulsory) to a highly organized timetable, there is far too little time available for private study and reading beyond the students' immediate course. Few courses prepare their students to understand, let alone take part in, educational research. This is to be regretted, for if a student is to remain critically aware of new techniques and methods during his teaching life, an ability to understand and interpret up-to-date research is essential.

A review of teaching methods in the colleges is urgent if we are to cease turning out students who are frustrated and dissatisfied with the quality of their education and training. 'To assume that children can be satisfactorily taught by teachers who themselves have been educationally frustrated . . . is a crime'[23].

The introduction of the Bachelor of Education degree is generally welcomed by students, but its present structure and form of administration is a cause of considerable anxiety. Apart from the fact that the present provision for the number of students to take the degree is totally inadequate to meet the demand, the B.Ed. has been introduced in a chaotic manner. As a consequence the distortions and inequalities of entry qualifications, syllabuses and status of the various degrees that have ensued have caused major difficulties. Students are frustrated and discontented about the future of the B.Ed., and rightly so. In some colleges there are 'three degrees in one' courses – education plus two academic subjects all simultaneously studied to degree level or higher. In others, all students follow the Certificate course for three years and then do what amounts to a year's cramming for the B.Ed. Neither situation is helpful or liked by the students. In some institutes, university matriculation requirements are demanded as an entry qualification to the B.Ed. course, at others the Teacher's Certificate, and still others require a special university examination to be taken by the prospective B.Ed. student. This only furthers confusion amongst prospective students endeavouring to select a college and course with which they can cope. Some institutes relegate education to a minor place in the B.Ed. syllabus, and a further differentiation occurs in the type of degree awarded by different institutes – some award only a pass or general degree while others award honours. All this is very unsatisfactory.

There can be no doubt what the majority of college-of-education students want for the Bachelor of Education degree. Firstly, entry qualifications should be uniform throughout the country and the Teacher's Certificate should form the basis of any matriculation requirement. Secondly, the B.Ed. courses should be 'education based', and so aimed at producing teachers who are more professionally qualified. Finally, a fully classified honours degree should be awarded in all cases.

The development of a critical frame of mind is something that is theoretically applauded in many colleges, but which is actively frowned upon in others. Conformity from students to an unrealistic and outmoded set of educational ideals seems to be the order of the day in these colleges:

Real open discussion and argument was rare, if only because lecturers showed time and time again that they were not really prepared to have their views openly scrutinized and criticized. In fact criticism of ideas was treated as personal criticism and as a challenge to the tutor's authority and hence it was often met by anger. Consistent dissenters were considered to be rude and immature. The students response to this situation was hardly surprising: they adapted, becoming pliant and accommodating keeping their real opinions to themselves and resignedly accepting their passive role[24].

The illiberal ordering and administration of many colleges is disturbing to their students. Petty rules and regulations all appear farcical in the light of what really matters – the education of professional practitioners able to cope with the continually changing character of modern schools.

Many people felt an enormous initial relief to be rid of the constrictive confines of a school-type education, but expressed profound disillusionment that their new environment was little different. . . . Petty and childish restrictions hinder any attempt at adult development.[25]

This is not an uncommon view of college-of-education life. In many colleges students are given little opportunity to carry individual or collective responsibility, and the concept inherent in the NUS/ATCDE (Association of Teachers in Colleges and Departments of Education) statement on college regulations[26] that students are co-equal partners of an adult community is often meaningless. When it is considered that these same students will, as soon as they leave the college, have the sole responsibility for the education of thirty to forty young people the situation is seen to be even more ludicrous. Issues such as the colour of men's shirts, the necessities of wearing a tie, the length of students' hair, and of women wearing slacks instead of skirts, take on an importance within some colleges that they clearly do not deserve. Although there are many students who react against this kind of regulation the system usually leaves its mark:

For many an able student it was an unhappy three years – years full of frustration. A great deal of the energy which students should have devoted to their studies and their own personal development was dissipated in the struggle with absurd rules and regulations . . . and it was generally the better students – usually the more sensitive ones – who made up their minds that if this was what the world of teaching was like, they would not stay in it for long[25].

There are still all-female colleges of education where members of the opposite sex, including fathers, are not allowed to visit students in their study-bedrooms. It is this kind of maternalistic regulation, along with other oppressive rules, that anger and frustrate so many students, and are a major cause of discontent.

One major problem that the colleges have yet to face is the

increasing number of students who arrive at their gates because it is the only avenue left open for them to enter higher education. They no longer represent the committed or dedicated student teachers. Charles Carter, Vice-Chancellor of Lancaster University, recently suggested that perhaps some 40 per cent of college-of-education students don't really wish to be there at all, and that if they could change their courses they would certainly do so. This view seems substantiated by a number of studies – the most recent was undertaken by Smithers and Carlisle – in which they labelled these students the 'reluctant teachers'[27]. They carried out a limited survey of third-year students at two northern colleges of education and asked the question: 'If you were quite free to choose and could obtain the qualifications necessary, what field of employment would you ideally like to enter?' Fifty-three per cent replied that they would like to enter some employement other than teaching. Similarly, at another progressive college of education 46·4 per cent of the students felt that they would teach temporarily or not at all on completing their training[28]. A college of education spokesman for the National Union of Students was recently reported as saying:

I think the vague myth that people in the colleges of education are dedicated has got to be dispelled for the colleges' own sake. Large numbers of students, I should say the majority, are not in any way committed to teaching in the sense in which people who teach in those colleges, or who look at those colleges from the outside, believe they are[29].

Clearly, the 'reluctant' student teachers are using the colleges as one of the few means open to them of furthering their own education. 'A picture emerges of a large number of reluctant teachers entering our colleges of education because they have nowhere else to go. Attracted to teaching by the time it affords for their family and leisure, they harbour doubts because it does not provide enough money to enjoy these to the full'[27].

An answer to many of the problems of structure referred to in this chapter might be the introduction of a consecutive course of training which would replace the present concurrent form, so providing the valuable flexibility needed to maximize the potential of each student. The students would opt for a professional training course only after completing their academic education.

To the students in the colleges of education, serious reform is needed now if the colleges are not only to fulfil their personal aspirations, but also to prepare them adequately for the schools of the future.

References

1. Summary notes on SPERTTT Conference, 25 October 1969.

2. National Young Teacher Advisory Committee of NUT, *The Future of Teacher Education*, 1969.

3. P. Marris, *The Experience of Higher Education*, Routledge & Kegan Paul, 1964.

4. NUT, 'Teacher education – the way ahead', discussion document, 1970.

5. P. Robinson, 'Student attitudes in a college of education', NUS, 1969.

6. NUS, *Colleges of Education: The Three-Year Course*, 1966.

7. Committee on Higher Education, 'Students and their education', in *Higher Education (Robbins Report)*, appendix 2(B), HMSO, 1963. See also National Young Teacher Advisory Committee of NUT, *The Future of Teacher Education*, 1969; NUT, 'Teacher education – the way ahead', discussion document, 1970; P. Robinson, 'Student attitudes in a college of education', NUS, 1969.

8. M. Shipman, 'The assessment of teaching practice', *Education for Teaching*, ATCDE, 1966.

9. G. Sorensen, 'What is learned in practice teaching?', *Research in Education*, November 1969.

10. M. Shipman, *Theory and Practice in the Education of Teachers*, *Education for Teaching*, ATCDE, 1967. See also H. T. Butcher, 'The attitudes of student teachers to education', *British Journal of Educational Psychology*, 1965.

11. E. A. Allen, 'The professional training of teachers', *Educational Research*, vol. 3, 1963.

12. National Young Teacher Advisory Committee of NUT, *The Future of Teacher Education*, 1969; P. Robinson, 'Student attitudes in a college of education', NUS, 1969; NUS, *Colleges of Education: The Three-Year Course*, 1966.

13. NUT, 'Teacher education – the way ahead', discussion document, 1970.

14. P. Robinson, 'Student attitudes in a college of education', NUS, 1969; Committee on Higher Education, 'Students and their education', in *Higher Education (Robbins Report)*, appendix 2(B), HMSO, 1963; NUS, *Colleges of Education: The Three-Year Course*, 1966.

15. P. Robinson, 'Student attitudes in a college of education', NUS, 1969.

16. NUS, 'Adjustments and failure', in *Memorandum to the Robbins Committee on Higher Education*, para. 53, 1961.

17. National Young Teacher Advisory Committee of NUT, *The Future of Teacher Education*, 1969.

18. National Young Teacher Advisory Committee of NUT, *The Future of Teacher Education*, 1969; NUS, *Colleges of Education: The Three-Year Course*, 1966; E. A. Allen, 'The professional training of teachers', *Educational Research*, vol. 3, 1963.

19. W. Taylor, *Society and the Education of Teachers*, Faber, 1969.

20. NUS, *Report of the Commission on Teaching in Higher Education*, 1969.

21. J. McLeish, *The Lecture Method*, Cambridge Institute of Education, 1968.

22. NUS, *Report of the Commission on Teaching in Higher Education*, 1969.

23. Summary notes on SPERTTT Conference, 25 October 1969.

24. C. Huxley, 'Who will teach the teachers?', *Peace News*, 10 October 1969.

25. *The Times Educational Supplement*, 19 March 1970.

26. NUS/ATCDE, *College Regulations on Residence*, 1965.

27. A. Smithers and S. Carlisle, 'Reluctant teachers', *New Society*, 5 March 1970.

28. P. Robinson, 'Student attitudes in a college of education', NUS, 1969.

29. 'It's your children they're teaching', BBC Radio 4 programme, 30 December 1969.

Part Two
Content and Commitment

3 The Values of Teacher Education
Danny McDowell

There is little point in discussing the administrative arrangements of any organization or institution without reference to
the values which underlie its work. There is a dynamic relationship between values and structure.

In the first place any particular set of administrative
arrangements embodies goals and hence values: a system of
comprehensive schools, for example, seeks equality of social and
educational opportunity. On the other hand, although a particular form of organization may be imposed and administered by
those who support the goals, those who work the system may
often produce unintended results because they perceive the
work in different terms or because they do not share the values
of the planners. Authoritarian attitudes, disguised social selection, an irrelevant curriculum may well be far more important
in determining what is actually achieved than the particular
form of organization.

There is an inevitable tendency for anyone working in an
organization, such as a school or college, to assume that its
purpose is self-evident. A headmaster might say that the goal
of his school is to 'educate our future citizens to take a responsible and active part in the community', but we all recognize
within that broad aim a multitude of implicit assumptions. We
would need to know a great deal about the society and the
community in which this particular school was situated in order
to have even a general notion of what our headmaster meant
by 'educate' or 'responsible and active part'. We would all
accept that this same statement made by the headmaster of a
public school and by the headmaster of a secondary-modern
school would be based upon very different assumptions about
the likely place of their pupils in society or even of the kind
of society which each anticipated. There are, then, both explicit

values, relating to the formal goals and aims of the organization, and implicit values which may conflict with the declared aims of the organization.

This chapter will attempt to examine the dynamic relationships between structure and values in teacher education. Its theme will be that teacher education rests on an inherited set of unexamined assumptions about the purpose of education and the nature of teaching which are largely irrelevant to contemporary schools and to the personal and professional needs of students. The system and its values are showing remarkable tenacity: first, because they have been left alone so long as they satisfied official criteria for success, criteria based on notions of crude productivity; and, second, because the imprecise state of knowledge in education encourages experience and spontaneity at the expense of systematic inquiry. After a period of great and unprecedented expansion in the colleges of education and an imminent re-examination of the whole structure and purpose of higher education, the colleges must examine with care their explicit assumptions and make explicit those which are implicit. If there is anything distinctive and valuable in the traditions of teacher education – and I believe that there is – then it ought to be the job of a national inquiry to identify these elements and to ensure their survival and effectiveness in any new arrangements suggested.

Unfortunately most of the pressures operating on teachers and teacher educators are opposed to any such process. The teacher's role is becoming increasingly diffuse as more, often conflicting, demands are made upon him and the schools, and as education has been faced with rising numbers, rising expectations and an unparalleled growth of knowledge. Consequently, as an American anthropologist, Fred Eggan, has pointed out, educators have been so busy coping with these expanding demands that they have had 'little time or opportunity to step outside their educational institutions and see them as a system in the society as a whole'[1]. It may not be too late for teacher educators to do this and critically to assess their work and its assumptions, which in turn would seem to imply ending the social and occupational isolation of colleges of education and to begin questioning the over-riding demands of central and local government for more teachers regardless of long-term educational and social needs.

Mass education – the missionary spirit

The broad value orientations of teacher education have their roots in the provision of mass elementary education. Until 1944 – and indeed well after – there were two kinds of publicly financed educational institutions in Britain, one for the mass of people and the other, quite distinct in organization and purpose, for the middle classes. We have not yet resolved what kind of secondary education is desirable for the majority of children – and there is no tradition of mass secondary education on which to draw. Compare the confidence with which the infant and junior age-group teacher is prepared with the uncertainty and ambivalence surrounding the secondary age-group courses.

Elementary education had a two-fold basis: 'The need to ensure discipline, and to obtain respect for private property and the social order, as well as to provide the kind of instruction which was indispensable in an expanding industrial and commercial nation' and 'To gentle the masses was another social purpose'[2]. The basic job was the bringing of social and personal betterment to the majority of children; this deep concern – characterized by Jean Floud as 'the missionary spirit'[3] – has evolved into what has been described as 'the semi-official ideology of the primary school'[4]: a view of the child, based on crude psychology, which is child-centred to the point of ignoring the whole social and economic structure which will determine his expectations and life chances. The teacher, in this context, is an agent of social consensus, not of social change; a man or woman imbued (hopefully) with a deep social and moral purpose which is to equip the unsuccessful majority to lead useful and moral lives within an established social and occupational structure. This tradition of social concern is just as potentially valuable and necessary in contemporary society as it was in the late nineteenth and first half of the twentieth century. Unfortunately, it supports and maintains a view of teaching and education which is ineffective and largely irrelevant; it assumes a society and an educational system which in fact have changed, are changing and will change at an accelerating pace. This rapid rate of change, which is the dominant characteristic of advanced industrialized societies, means that: 'The school is now preparing children for a cultural situation which it cannot adequately foresee. It must concentrate therefore upon preparing the pupils with tools (techniques and values) for handling unknown situations'[5].

In such a situation the role of the teacher, as modelled in the colleges of education, is inappropriate. This role emphasizes good personal relationships, if necessary at the expense of effective teaching[6], and values experience as the best teacher.

The argument is not with good personal relationships: many children need to develop trust and even affection for the teacher before they can begin to learn; nor is it with the intention to improve the quality of life for children and for the community; but rather with the notion that good relationships and right feelings are enough. Dorothy Emmett, a philosopher, has defined the problem well in relation to social work and social values:

... and certainly 'help' nowadays cannot be effectively given merely by goodwill. Apart from the fact that effective remedies for social distress may call for political measures, help for people's individual and personal difficulties calls for expert skills. ... Thus the giving of help becomes dependent on acquiring certain kinds of expert knowledge and skill[7].

The teacher is not encouraged by his education to think and function in terms of specific technical skills and, hence, a specific (and manageable) role for himself. Teachers are ill-placed and ill-served by their education and training when it comes to coping with and assessing the increasing, often conflicting, demands being made on them. How can they effectively combine the roles of moral tutor, teacher of subjects and skills, and that of social worker? In the last few years they have also been urged by a variety of interested organizations to accept responsibility for the child's competence as a cyclist, pedestrian and car driver; for his sexual competence; for his political education; for the child as consumer; for his knowledge and resistance to drugs, cigarettes and alcohol – and so on. If all the individuals and organizations who have made demands on teachers' time, skills and energy were to be satisfied, teachers could be fully employed even without teaching any of the traditional curriculum.

These diverse demands and expectations of teachers and of education are a reflection of our greatly heightened awareness of the complex inter-relationships of education and the social and economic structure of our society; they also reflect a rapid rate of social change, but great uncertainty as to how schools should relate to it. Should they reflect it? Should they attempt to initiate it? Or have educators consistently overestimated the impact of education on society? The consequence for the teacher is that there is uncertainty built into everything he does. Should he attempt to satisfy his clients? But who are his clients? Are they his pupils or those who employ him? And who are his employers? Is it parents or the local education authority or society?

The consequence for the child is that his school experience will be full of inconsistencies and contradictions. He will rarely, except perhaps in the primary school, encounter a learning situation which is consistent in its content, aims and mood. To ask a group of secondary-school teachers what they think their job is about is quickly to reveal confusion, uncertainty and contradictions. None of this is surprising when the colleges provide a training which is neither thoroughly professional nor intellectually stimulating, and which leaves the young teacher no alternative but to adopt the ideas and attitudes of the older classroom teacher who has evolved for himself a working relationship with the children, with his colleagues and with 'the school'. Not surprisingly the essentially liberal and reformist ideas of the colleges are seen in retrospect as irrelevant to the real job in hand.

What has been said here is an attempt to give a context to the discussion which follows of the internal life of the colleges and to a plea that colleges examine their assumptions and aims. If they do not they will be ill-prepared to defend their work and existence against those who would make them the whipping boy for all the shortcomings of the schools. The attacks will come, in the main, from people with little regard for, and less understanding of, the past and potential contribution of teacher training in this country, a contribution provided despite the callous manipulation of the system in order to produce teachers as quickly and as cheaply as possible.

The internal life of the colleges
'There are no issues'

The key to understanding what is happening within the colleges now is to see them as organizations, driven by their situation to accept rapid growth but prevented by their basic value orientations from accepting and using the changes and possibilities which could follow.

The view taken of the teacher's role means that the colleges attempt to develop in their students a degree of commitment to their future job which will generate the social and moral purpose which the job traditionally demands. The emphasis, therefore, must be on 'relationships between teachers and pupils', the focus 'as a child-centred rather than a subject-centred activity'[8]. There tends to be an emphasis on those 'academic' subjects – literature, history, drama and religious studies – which can best support the romantic tradition of English education, a concern with human values and 'large questions of social purpose'. It would seem extraordinary, given the position of education as a determinant of personal and economic progress, that there is not yet a college of education with a department of politics or economics. Professor William Taylor points out that the traditional concern of the colleges with 'social purpose' and human values is reflected in discussions of social problems presented not in terms of 'the major structural and economic features of society – the class system, the effects of the division of labour and industrialization on the distribution of income', but in terms of 'the less significant and peripheral aspects of the working of these larger structures – the "waste makers", the "hidden persuaders", the "status seekers" and the "pyramid climbers" of society'[9].

The education courses in colleges have a core of child development rather than educational psychology, which does not lend itself so easily to the development of the 'semi-official ideology of the primary school'. This is supported by some kind of teaching in philosophy, sociology and history of education, which for some inexplicable reason always seems to begin with the Dame Schools of the seventeenth century and end with the 1944 Education Act. The student is expected to make some kind of synthesis of these very diverse elements – all subsumed under the title 'educational theory' – usually taught by staff with little or no training in the basic disciplines. The education course, more than any other element in the college curriculum, is designed – albeit unconsciously – as a means of inculcating commitment in the student. As we have said, teaching is presented as an exercise in good personal relationships. The educational theory is taught selectively rather than thoroughly, so as to emphasize those elements which will stress the diffuse aspects of the job: there is not even an attempt to define the specific elements in teaching. It often amounts to little more than 'a miscellany of ideas about the aims of education in the light of which, it is at least implied and probably explicitly stated, [the teacher] must arrive at his own notion of what his job entails and the aims he must pursue'[10]. The staff of the education departments of colleges are in an invidious position. They represent that element in the colleges which is closest to the schools, and yet the majority of them will have had no recent – say within three years – experience of school teaching; very few will have graduate qualifications in their area of educational theory; they tend to be rather unsuccessful hybrids, uncertain of their loyalty and with little status among staff or students.

School practice, the third major element in the student's college course, is almost deliberately made into a traumatic experience; he is about to 'do' the real thing. Teaching practice assessment will normally stress good personal relationships with both pupils and staff; ability to cooperate, and neatness of dress; clarity of speech; classroom organization and a 'good' set of lesson notes. It may also stress knowledge of subject, and indications of effectiveness in teaching a particular lesson or lessons. Ultimately the decisive impression left on the supervising tutor will be in terms of relationship with the class, relationship with individual children and ability to cooperate. It is likely that the 'successful' student is one who is skilful in presenting the right 'image' both in tutorials and on teaching practice.

68 Content and Commitment

Students all too clearly regard the bulk of what happens in college as a stylized procedure devised by conscientious but ineffective do-gooders. Writers on teacher education have suggested that there are two frames of reference for students in colleges, one a 'college frame of reference' involving close agreement between students and tutors about pupil–teacher relationships, the other a 'school frame of reference' involving 'less idealized views of teacher–pupil relations or classroom experience'[11].

Yet another writer has suggested that students give an 'onstage' response for the benefit of tutors but maintain quite different beliefs among themselves[12]. Donald Lomax (see Chapter 1) shows us clearly how the 'real' frame of reference of the students is external to the college; their interest and values do not coincide at any point with the intentions of the college. The students' main point of reference is the social group to which he belongs outside the college; these social groups 'insulate their members against the purposes and values of the larger organization'[13]. Students, particularly the more able, are interested in and concerned with ideas. The concern with vocational skills, with its emphasis on received truth, is at variance with the students' need for a wide-ranging intellectual diet. Disassociation from the purposes and values of the college is likely to increase as the colleges attract large numbers of young people whose major priority is their own personal higher education.

In the colleges they find institutions which have not resolved whether they are offering a higher liberal or a vocational education. They find forms of teaching and assessment which assume a dichotomy between education and training, between intellectual activity, valuable experience and moral concern – a syndrome well expressed by an American, Richard Hofstadter:

Intellect is pitted against feeling, on the ground that it is somehow inconsistent with warm emotion. It is pitted against character, because it is widely believed that intellect stands for mere cleverness, which transmutes easily into the sly or the diabolical. It is pitted against practicality, since theory is held to be opposed to practice, and the 'purely' theoretical mind is so much disesteemed. It is pitted against democracy, since intellect is thought to be a form of distinction that defies egalitarianism[14].

As a consequence students are denied access to academic knowledge and insights which alone can give meaning and purpose to
the techniques of professional education. The provision of a
liberal education for teachers in training is not possible where
so much time is spent, largely under the heading of educational
theory, on the indoctrination of students – a process which is
probably ineffective and clearly at variance with the views of
practising teachers. Of course students need practical skills for
classroom use and, of course, they should develop a sympathetic relationship with those they teach, but it will avail nothing unless they have confidence and flexibility of mind and an
academic education which will be a basis for forty years of
teaching.

These problems and the assumptions underlying them are
enshrined in the concurrent course. The insistence on concurrent training, given official and confused blessing in the *Eighth
Report of the National Council on the Training and Supply of
Teachers*, has its roots in the need, already discussed, to give
teachers a particular view of teaching. In practical terms it
means an overlapping of time and function of the personal
education of the student (main course work), of work in educational theory, and of the teaching-practice element. This leads
to fragmented timetables and endless possibilities for conflict
between the academic departments and the department of education. The student, and particularly the good student, loses
heavily; he undergoes a conflict of loyalties to different areas
of work and different philosophies of what teaching is about,
and he may never find substantial time in which to read, think
and discuss anything which fires his imagination or which seems
particularly relevant to his future career. The consequence is
that the bulk of students – and the process is noticeable at the
beginning of the second year – settle for a policy of meeting
their minimum commitments; their intellectual and academic
interests and enthusiasms are saved for the pub or digs.

The methods of teaching are still, in many colleges, based on
what has been called 'the mother-hen principle' – small groups
of students under a single tutor.

These groups often attempt to generate emotional bonds in the

hope that understandings will be reached that are based on affect-
ivity, rather than objective facts or scientific theories of social behaviour. Here the authority of the group tutor is not based on his
superior knowledge or learning but his experience on moral good-
ness [15].

This 'manipulative socialization' is reflected in most other
areas of college life. Despite the need for increasing bureaucra-
tization most colleges still prefer to run administration on a
personal staff–student basis: it is not unusual to find routine
administrative information being conveyed to students through
an elaborate personal tutor system. The ideal principal is one
who 'knows' or has met every student. There is a determined
effort to avoid issues of success or failure; the system caters
for the 'C' student. There is a recognized vocabulary of euphe-
misms to describe those who fail – 'unsuitable for teaching' or
'withdrew for personal reasons'; there is a great reluctance to
admit a differentiation of work among staff or students. Recent
student demands in many colleges for 'the right to fail' caused
considerable embarrassment.

Community life is still regarded as an essential element in
college life: 'residential accommodation plays a great part in
contributing to the character of training college'[16]. Today, even
in large colleges with a minority of students in residence, those
staff who are themselves resident and act as wardens are seen
as guardians of the tradition of the college, and often enjoy
a prestige higher than their formal position in the staff hierarchy
would seem to justify. There is regret at the passing of the small
residential community where personal contact could meet most
administrative needs and where consensus and good relationships are easily maintained. A consensus arrived at by open
debate and awareness that there exist power relationships within any organization is a very different thing to a consensus
arrived at (or imposed?) because no one is prepared to raise
fundamental issues or because no one has a clear notion of
what the fundamental issues are. In such an ethos there is no
place for fundamental disagreement, which is interpreted as a
question of loyalty or of preventing what is known as 'getting
on with the real job'. There is an impatience with politics and
political issues, a relentless search for consensus which makes

the colleges easy prey for tough councillors and ensures long and disorganized staff and academic board meetings. Ideally there are no issues in the college of education, only local difficulties which, given goodwill and common sense, can be resolved.

External controls
'Responsibility without power'

There are a number of external pressures on the colleges which serve to preserve the system and its assumptions. First and foremost are the demands of central and local government.

The demand for teachers ... exercises an immediate and pressing influence upon the work of the colleges, which tends to take precedence over other educational considerations; during the post-war years, as we shall see, there has been an almost continuous conflict between considerations of the demands for and supply of teachers on the one hand and, on the other, the interests of teacher education in providing an improved personal and vocational education and in upgrading their educational and social status[17].

The Department of Education and Science and its junior partners, the local education authorities, have ruthlessly used the colleges as forcing grounds for more teachers. In order to retain the degree of social (that is political) control necessary to ensure productivity, the Government rejected the recommendations of the Robbins Committee on the administrative future of the colleges of education and has discouraged diversity in size and range of courses. Within the last few years there has emerged an unofficial policy of restricting the growth of major colleges, so that all colleges will fall within narrow limits of size and quality; nothing has been done to make possible the diversification of training recommended by the *McNair Report* of 1943 and by Robbins in 1963.

In short, official concern with crude productivity has a vested interest in maintaining the social and educational isolation of teacher education, in discouraging heterogeneity of size and function – all of which serves to insulate the colleges from the conflicts and demands and questioning which characterize other areas of higher education. There has been a convenient interaction of values and demand. The colleges have been left undisturbed and unquestioned as long as they have satisfied the logistical concern of the authorities and, in turn, the preoccupations and apolitical values of the colleges have encouraged this kind of expectation by the authorities. Whilst denying to the colleges any real autonomy or a wider brief, the Department of Education and Science has not given any educational lead; the colleges, until very recently, have been sheltered from public gaze and no MP has shown any consistent interest in their work. The civil servants and local-authority officials have evolved policy between them with little chance of being successfully challenged. The colleges have been given responsibility without power.

The colleges are administered and controlled by a mixture of 'advice' and bullying. Unlike the universities, the colleges receive their income on an annual basis; their recurrent expenditure from the local education authority is not even given as a global sum, which a college may spend as it sees best in the light of changing needs. Capital expenditure – new building projects and the like – are subject to the approval of the Department of Education and Science and it is largely this element which determines the size and rate of growth of each college. The *Weaver Report* gave to the academic board of each college responsibility for its academic work; but this is a hollow victory. Given the detailed and day-to-day control of the Department of Education and Science and of the local authority no academic board is free to plan and initiate a completely new type of course – it must first negotiate with the controlling bodies and with the school of education to which it belongs. The system of control and the manner in which it is exercised are such that the colleges have been denied sufficient autonomy and authority to develop the degree of confidence necessary if they are to innovate and extend themselves.

Of the other external pressures which serve to reinforce and maintain the traditional assumptions of teacher education, the most important is that exercised by the NUT and more broadly by a whole range of opinion represented by practising teachers generally and headmasters in particular. This pressure can be seen within the colleges – usually emanating from the education departments –and at every level of the teachers' unions. It was recently given official backing by Edward Short (when Secretary of State). This pressure takes the form of a demand that the colleges lay much more emphasis on the practical elements in teacher education and that 'practising teachers' (a magic phrase) should be much more closely involved in the education of teachers; it springs from 'the narrow notions of professionalism and the excessive concern with the minutiae of the pedagogical process and method of teaching'[18]. It is a reflection of the anti-intellectualism, the over-riding regard for experience, and the belief that good relationships at every level can provide answers to the most intransigent problems.

It may well be, of course, that practising teachers should be closely involved in the education of teachers – but in what capacity and to what end? If, as has been suggested, 'the [school] staff room is probably one of the most potent forces for conservatism in English education'[19], the demand by teachers for a bigger say in teacher education is at least suspect. But whatever the case for or against, the disturbing factor is that teacher involvement – and the values it implies – are taken as a self-evident truth by the bulk of the staff in the colleges. Another truth held to be self-evident by tutors and by serving teachers is that all staff in the colleges of education should have had substantial teaching experience in schools. What a dismal view this implies of the educational needs of teachers, that a young graduate, who stimulates and opens the minds of students, is not making a greater contribution to the education and professional competence of student teachers than an ex-deputy headmaster who left schools fifteen years ago and hasn't read a serious book since! But then if experience is all you have, experience is what you value.

Changes in the colleges and some proposals

But, of course, the colleges are changing; it is all too easy to talk of *changing the colleges* and to miss what may well be far more significant – *change in the colleges*. A large number of young and very different staff has been drawn into the colleges in the last ten years – staff who question the value orientations of the colleges and, in particular, the assumed consensus. There is probably now a nucleus of staff in every college, mainly under thirty-five and often with teaching experience in comprehensive schools or further education, who reject the view of education and of society implied in the work and organization of the college. The increasing size of colleges means that consensus is increasingly difficult to maintain.

A small number of able and male principals have been appointed in the past few years. It will be interesting to see how far and how quickly they can take their colleges, given the generally traditionalist views and narrow sympathies of college governors – still disappointingly dominated by local councillors or churches.

College-of-education students are at last beginning to ask radical questions; for the first time students from the colleges are playing a significant part in the National Union of Students, and that body has possibly done as much as any other to promote public debate about teacher education and its place in higher education.

Our main theme of irrelevant and value-laden teaching and organization is still valid, as is the colleges' deep-seated concern for the majority and the underprivileged. What we must quarrel with is the effectiveness of this concern when translated into the context of a highly diverse, political, industrial society. What can be done to make this concern more relevant and effective without losing the tradition of concern itself? Bearing in mind that the unintended consequences of any reorganization or change of perspective are probably as important as the intended ones, it would seem reasonable to suggest the following:

1. Maintain the colleges but make them much larger, say a minimum of 2000 students. Greatly extend the range of courses but not in the direction of providing B.A. (general) degrees, which would be an easy but irrelevant innovation.

2. End the concurrent course. Provide a two- or three-year liberal education with some emphasis on the social sciences (the two are not incompatible). The third or fourth year would be an extension of the present probationary year but with the school and college having a joint concern for the student

teacher. After the completion of his initial year the student would become a qualified teacher. As a basis for promotion, either to a more senior post *and/or* a higher salary scale, he would be required to attend, not later than five years after 'graduation', a year's in-service course, which would consist largely of educational theory weighted to support the areas of teaching (or social work) to which he had become committed – or to which he wished to commit himself in future.

Such a scheme would enable the two or three different elements in the present teacher-education programme to be defined more sharply and with more attainable aims, thus providing more satisfaction for staff and students alike. There could well be more interchange of staff and ideas within the college; a lecturer in sociology might give the bulk of his time to the initial education of the students but would also be involved in the in-service courses, focusing on educational theory, for experienced teachers. The initial year in school would need to be given great weight and would demand much rethinking about assessment and the aims of teaching – both of which would be the joint responsibility of school and college staff. A scheme of this type would provide a very real role for the experienced teacher who, instead of having to defend himself in a philosophy or psychology of education tutorial, would fill a central role of liaison between college and school; he would be the man who would synthesize the college lecture room and school classroom experience of the student teacher.

Above all, the student would be enabled to go into schools with a mind uncluttered by the confused expectations of what his job ought to be, but aware that his first four or five years of teaching were a learning situation for himself as well as his pupils; aware also that he would be able to return to college or a university and refine his experience of teaching by exposing it to a scientific and more theoretical perspective in the company of other teachers.

The development of in-service courses on a large scale is a prerequisite for radical change in the way we prepare teachers. If it can accompany a more specialized and more rational approach by the colleges, it should be possible to develop a clearer purpose which will give to the college-educated teacher the authority and flexibility so urgently needed in a profession at the centre of all social change.

References

1. F. Eggan, 'Social anthropology and the educational system', *School Review*, vol. 65, 1957, p. 247.

2. D. V. Glass, 'Education and social change in modern England', in A. H. Halsey and J. Floud (eds.), *Education, Economy and Society*, Collier-Macmillan, 1961, p. 394.

3. J. Floud, 'Teaching in the affluent society', *Year Book of Education 1963*, 1963, ch. 1, sect 3, p. 382.

4. B. Bernstein and B. Davies, 'Some sociological comments on Plowden', in R. S. Peters (ed.), *Perspectives on Plowden*, Routledge & Kegan Paul, 1969, p. 56.

5. D. F. Swift, *The Sociology of Education*, Routledge & Kegan Paul, 1970, p. 84.

6. For an interesting discussion of this point see F. Musgrove and P. H. Taylor, *Society and the Teacher's Role*, Routledge & Kegan Paul, 1969.

7. D. Emmett, 'Ethics and the social worker', in E. Younghusband (ed.), *Social Work and Social Values*, Allen & Unwin, 1967.

8. W. Taylor, *Society and the Education of Teachers*, Faber, 1969, p. 275.

9. W. Taylor, *Society and the Education of Teachers*, Faber, 1969, p. 283.

10. F. Musgrove and P. H. Taylor, *Society and the Teacher's Role*, Routledge & Kegan Paul, 1969, p. 9.

11. D. S. Finlayson and L. Cohen, 'The teacher's role: a comparative study of the conceptions of college of education students and headteachers', *British Journal of Educational Psychology*, vol. 37, 1967, p. 37.

12. M. Shipman, 'Personal and social influence on the work of a teachers' training college', Ph.D. thesis, London University, 1966.

13. M. Trow, 'Recruitment to college teaching', in A. H. Halsey and J. Floud (eds.), *Education, Economy and Society*, Collier-Macmillan, 1961, p. 614.

14. R. Hofstadter, *Anti-Intellectualism in American Life*, Cape, 1964, p. 46.

15. W. Taylor, *Society and the Education of Teachers*, Faber, 1969, p. 295.

16. *Ministry of Education Bulletin*, no. 15, HMSO, 1957.

17. W. Taylor, *Society and the Education of Teachers*, Faber, 1969, p. 32.

18. B. Holmes, G. Z. F. Bereday and J. A. Lauwerys, 'The education and training of teachers', in J. A. Lauwerys (ed.), *Teachers and Teaching*, Evans, 1969.

19. F. Musgrove and P. H. Taylor, *Society and the Teacher's Role*, Routledge & Kegan Paul, 1969, p. 9.

4 A Curriculum for Teacher Education
Peter Renshaw

The structure of the curriculum

The main purpose of this chapter is to examine the curriculum for the initial training of the 80 per cent of teachers who are non-graduates[1], most of whom teach in primary schools. My thesis is that although the existing system was carefully conceived initially, recent social, economic and technological pressures have placed new demands on teacher education. Increased knowledge from the findings of educational research and mounting professional pressure from the teachers' unions are forcing teacher educators to rethink what they are doing. Two central questions need to be asked. Does the system lack a positive sense of direction? And secondly, can the existing structures cope with the changed circumstances?

The present three-year Certificate course is offered mainly in mono-vocational colleges of education. It consists of three areas of study:

1. One or two main subjects which are said to be designed for the 'personal development' of the student and modelled in many cases on the traditional pattern of the university honours school.

2. Curriculum or professional courses intended to enable students to teach a wide range of subjects.

3. The theory and practice of education.

This basic structure was introduced for the two-year course in 1949 at the Standing Conference of Area Training Organizations[2]. With this pattern emerged a new set of problems which partly form the basis of current dissatisfaction with college courses.

But before raising points of criticism, it must be acknowledged that for far too long teacher training was regarded as an inferior and impoverished sector of the educational system. It had to endure a lengthy struggle to attain recognition as part of higher education. This was hardly surprising since the 'pupil–teacher' system, which dominated colleges from 1840 to 1890, was not likely to gladden the heart of the traditional university academic. Students were subjected to a vast array of courses[3], and the emphasis on teaching method and mechanical teaching techniques resulted in a narrow stereotyped training. But in defence of the colleges, they did have to compensate for a non-existent system of national elementary education until 1870, and even up to 1902 they had to fill the gap left by the inadequate provision of secondary education.

Teacher training, then, hardly got off to a propitious start, and it is not surprising to see the gradual strengthening of the relationship between universities and training colleges once the day training colleges were established in 1890. But the influence of the universities on college curriculum and academic standards was slow to gain momentum. Up to 1949 there was a conspicuous lack of change in the structure of the curriculum, which continued to be overcrowded by a large number of unrelated professional and general subjects. Courses were intellectually undemanding due to a concept of 'professional training' dating back to the nineteenth century. But a ray of hope entered with the publication of the *McNair Report* on *Teachers and Youth Leaders* (1944), which recommended:

1. A closer relationship between universities and colleges through the establishment of Area Training Organizations and Institutes of Education.

2. The desirability of students pursuing one subject in greater depth.

3. Raising the academic standard of the education course.

4. The need to achieve a balance between academic and professional studies.

5. A more realistic teaching-practice system based on the 'apprenticeship' model.

6. The extension of the college course to three years, with one year's probation after qualification.

The *McNair Report* acted as a catalyst. The resulting closer link with the universities enabled the colleges to raise their sights, and their first move was to introduce the main subject, which was designed 'primarily for its value in the personal development of the student and not necessarily having any direct connection with his teaching work'[4]. Once the present pattern was established in 1949 the focus of discussion shifted towards the extension of the course to three years, in an attempt to raise the standards of both academic and professional studies and to bring the training colleges more in line with the universities. The *Fifth* and *Sixth Reports of the National Advisory Council on the Training and Supply of Teachers* were devoted to the idea of a three-year course[5], as was the Ministry of Education's *The Training of Teachers*[6]. When the new Certificate course finally materialized in 1960, the partnership between colleges and universities, although remaining unequal, was further cemented. This was especially evident in the design of the main subject, which took the traditional university undergraduate course somewhat uncritically as its model.

Today we must question whether this was appropriate for an area of study which was quickly to assume a dominant position in a *teacher education* curriculum. It can be appreciated that the main subject added some academic weight to a Certificate which had in the past been bedevilled by a multiplicity of low-level content and method courses[7]. But its character and status could not but reinforce the growing separation between academic and professional studies in colleges. Gradually the academic education of the student became associated with the main subject, whilst the study of curriculum courses and education was identified as professional training. In many cases, no doubt, a desire for academic prestige unduly influenced the colleges to ape universities. But would it not have been more pertinent for them to have developed in their own distinctive way, establishing a curriculum best suited to achieve their own ends? A college of education should be a unique institution set up to educate and train potential teachers, encouraged to pursue its own individual ends rather than to imitate the university.

However, the structure of the college curriculum has continued to be dominated by traditional university thinking, encouraged in this by the Association of Teachers in Colleges and Departments of Education (ATCDE) and endorsed by the

Robbins Committee on *Higher Education* (1963), which proposed the new B.Ed. degree[8]. The recent dialogue between
universities and colleges not only concerns the four-year degree
course, but could also have far-reaching effects on the standards and character of the Certificate course. For instance, the
main subject could continue in an academic strait-jacket with
little professional relevance; the demands of the B.Ed. might
cast its shadow back and constrict imaginative curriculum
developments; a closer link between education and subject departments might be impeded. In addition the structure of the
education course could radically alter with the recent differentiated conception of educational theory, which has enabled the
study of education to be truly academic, through its contribu-
tory disciplines of philosophy, psychology, sociology and
history[9].

It must not be thought that I am suggesting that a conspiracy
existed between the universities, the ATCDE and the hierarchy
in colleges. Whatever social pressures may have propelled the
colleges into the university arena, educationally their intentions were sound in the context of the period. We needed, and
still do need, better educated teachers to give children a more
worth-while education. Academic standards were deplorably
low and the whole status of colleges within the structure of
higher education needed to be raised. But there comes a time
when any system must be reviewed. Changes have occurred
during the last decade, but has the thinking underlying the
present curriculum been sufficiently fundamental? Are existing structures relevant to current needs or are they constrained
by a pseudo-academic parochialism?

Such questions need to be asked, because any college curriculum must be geared to producing teachers who can understand
the demands of education and society in a rapidly changing
world. It is little wonder that there is growing uncertainty about
the validity of the present curriculum[10], for we ought to be
training teachers to prepare children for a highly complex
technologically based economy, in which they would be capable
of coping with and generating change. The children of today
are entering a dynamic 'regenerative society'[11], in which the
pace of technological advance is accelerating, bringing in its

wake a range of new social and economic demands, new organizational structures, new concepts, attitudes, systems, roles and patterns of behaviour. The needs of such a society must be reflected in any teacher-education programme. Colleges cannot afford to be bound by obstructionist traditions; the curriculum should be continually reappraised in the light of ever-changing conditions.

A need for change is for the most part recognized, although there is disagreement about the direction it should take. For instance, in some colleges change is too frequently dominated by the 'prestige' links with the university, internal and external vested interests, irrelevant formal requirements and transitory practical demands. Moreover, evidence is mounting to demonstrate a sharp cleavage within some institutions over the structure of courses and the growing dichotomy between academic and professional studies. There are those who wish to make a fundamental examination of the curriculum from first principles, whilst others confine their conception of change to the rehabilitation of existing structures. Such differing viewpoints, often based on conflicting value-systems, tend to make communication tenuous and positive growth almost impossible.

What are some of the central areas that need to be examined? First a clear statement of the objectives of teacher education needs to be formulated. Total consensus may never be reached, but at present these goals are diffuse and poorly conceptualized. Without carefully conceived objective criteria how can we expect to achieve rational curriculum planning? Another possible impediment to reform is that the curriculum is geared to a single 'common qualification', a principle strongly upheld by the NUT[12]. But the notion of 'a teacher', who by virtue of his training can fit into any teaching job, is a limiting principle for curriculum change, particularly when the college curriculum is viewed against the diffuse nature of the student body, with its diversity of ability, interests and destinations. A common certificate may give the profession some sort of unity, but I would maintain that a much stronger sense of 'professionalism' could be gained by a body of more highly skilled and knowledgeable teachers operating in specialist areas – whether it be in a reception class or a sixth form. People would be respected as authorities in specific areas, and flexibility attained through retraining schemes and in-service 'adjustment' courses. In other words, in a college it might be more appropriate to conceive of different lengths and types of training planned in relation to a differentiated teaching force in which the student is trained to carry out a specific function[13].

This view challenges the value of the main course for every student. But is the traditional main academic subject or a more general education more beneficial for teachers of young children? The whole structure and status of the main subject needs to be questioned, instead of perpetuating the myth that it has a monopoly of academic study and is the only area of the curriculum that contributes to the 'personal development' of the student[14]. This leads us to ask further questions concerning the relatively undifferentiated programmes for primary and secondary students. Are the present categories (e.g. infant, junior, secondary) of students logical? Not only are many local education authorities beginning to reorganize their schools on the lines suggested by the Plowden Committee[15], but the first, middle and secondary classification could be considered more appropriate on both logical and psychological grounds. If so, should a first-school student teacher receive the same education and training as one intending to teach in a middle or secondary school? Finally, if the professional component of the curriculum were re-examined from first principles, would the present proliferation of traditional curriculum courses stand up to critical scrutiny?

A critique of the present structure of the college of education curriculum
The need for a clear statement of curriculum objectives

As I suggested earlier, the present system of teacher education lacks a positive sense of direction, and the structure of its curriculum fails in many ways to reflect the academic and professional demands of a rapidly developing profession. Objectives must be clearly articulated and mutually consistent, thus enabling a range of coherent strategies to be conceived within a broad conceptual framework.

But the complexity of the situation in schools and colleges

makes this task far from straightforward. For instance, the growing diffuseness of the teacher's role, the wide range of academic, technological and practical demands, varying criteria for evaluating students and conflicting values within the profession – all these factors make it difficult to draw up a job specification for teachers that could form the basis of a rational, viable programme. Nevertheless, it is possible to pinpoint some of the qualities that the profession will be demanding from the teacher of the future.

One of the most marked developments is that the concept of the teacher is changing. There has been a growing move away from the traditional formal lesson directed to a single class. Now that the child is seen as the centre of the learning process, the teacher has to participate in a variety of positive ways. Not only does he have to instruct, but he has to understand how to structure learning experiences with the emphasis on flexible approaches, individual and group work, providing suitable conditions and materials for intended learning. With the advent of team teaching, a teacher may well be one link in a complex, structually differentiated teaching force comprising leader teachers, specialist teachers, teacher assistants and technicians. These developments mean that he will have to become professionally more informed and to gain more elaborate organizational and management expertise. The teacher no longer just 'teaches', in the instructional sense. The diverse nature and demands of our advanced industrial society have opened up a range of responsibilities for schools including the education and socialization of children, social welfare and counselling, educational measurement and testing.

What are the implications of this for colleges? First, probably more than ever before, student teachers must develop a heightened sensitivity to the needs of individual children. This is particularly necessary because of the sort of society in which we live, and the curriculum must help to draw out the dynamic relationship between school and society. Secondly, in order to make responsible judgements and reasoned decisions, students must build up a wide range of conceptual understanding and skills, including the ability to cope with radical changes in the technology and methodology of teaching. The capacity to preserve an autonomy of mind based on reason and knowledge is essential in a period of rapid expansion and change. It would be hoped that a curriculum would try to foster in students an objective, critical attitude towards educational innovation, which will enable them to evaluate the changing conception of teaching and research findings. Moreover, because of the changing structure and status of the profession, the teacher of the future must develop an occupational consciousness, which should include political, economic and sociological dimensions. A teacher-education programme, then, must aim at producing self-confident, self-critical, adaptable and technically competent teachers who satisfy certain agreed public standards.

But such specifications must not be left at this high level of generality. To be effective guides for action they must be refined and reformulated in more specific operational terms. Each college needs to translate such general principles into a viable teaching programme. I would urge that the conceptualization of objectives is an essential precondition of rational curriculum planning. Many recent small changes in colleges seem to have lacked any obvious underlying rationale, and in most cases fundamental structural reform has been sacrificed for piecemeal timetable engineering. What we must do now is to examine the function of several existing structures and to offer suggestions for possible new lines of development.

Academic study in a college of education

As I suggested earlier, there is a conviction in colleges that the main subject has a monopoly of academic study and that it is the only area of the curriculum that contributes to the 'personal development' of the student. But why must the idea of personal development be limited to the main subject? Isn't it relevant to other aspects of the college curriculum and to the total life of the institution?

The notion of personal development partly suggests that a person is being initiated into a whole range of experiences that help to develop him as a centre of consciousness. As he deepens his understanding and 'gets inside' an activity he develops certain attitudes, qualities of mind, values and beliefs as to what is worth-while. This knowledge enables him to make responsible rational choices. His search for reasons as to why he should act in certain ways leads to the demand for justifications for all activities; he is no longer dependent on some external, and perhaps irrational, authority. In other words, through a person's commitment to an activity, his central concern becomes the search for truth and the development of personal autonomy based on reason.

But, although rational autonomy is central to a student's intellectual development, other qualities are also significant if he is to gain the balanced personality and the breadth of maturity so necessary for teaching. For instance, emotional stability, self-control, self-awareness, the ability to establish interpersonal relationships and the capacity to act rationally – all form part of the development of a person, but they will hardly be acquired through the academic study of one main subject, or even through a range of subjects. The development of such qualities requires not only a variety of teaching experiences with children, but also an 'open' atmosphere in the college, with a wide range of liberalizing experiences aimed at maturing the students as people, broadening their outlook and giving them a realistic understanding of the world outside teaching.

Undoubtedly, the objective study of a subject pursued in depth for its own sake can contribute to the personal development of the student. Such study involves 'getting inside' a discipline in an attempt to master its methods of inquiry, to understand the distinctive nature of the activity, and to see how it relates to other areas of knowledge. This sort of academic study helps to develop such qualities of mind as rationality, autonomy, judgement, imagination, critical and logical thinking, but these qualities can be viewed only in relation to a specific discipline[16]. Historical judgement, for instance, is logically distinct from aesthetic or scientific judgement. Imagination in literature is different in kind from imagination in physics or history. Since no discipline can develop these qualities *in general*, the experiences gained from studying one main subject can contribute only to a small part of a student's personal development.

The idea of personal development, then, embraces both academic and professional study, and includes those experiences gained from extra-curricular activities and the life of the institution in general. The notion of 'academic study' is limited in its scope, but not so limited as to be identified solely with the main subject. For instance, it also has a significant role in the theoretical study of education and in certain elements of the curriculum courses. Furthermore, because of the nature of the institution, as conceived at present, all academic study in a college of education has professional significance; it ought not to be pursued for intrinsic reasons alone[17]. A sharp dichotomy between the education and training of the student need not arise if a close relationship be maintained between academic and professional studies, and if it is understood that academic study need not stand in isolation, but is in fact an integral part of professional study.

If student teachers are to cultivate a self-critical appraisal of their teaching and a flexibility in response to educational innovation, if they are to develop autonomy, discrimination and the breadth of vision necessary for making responsible professional judgements, they require a general education which must be gained through academic study conceived within a professional frame of reference. Implicit, then, in a college of education programme is a close interrelationship between academic and professional studies. But does this crucial link exist in most colleges?

The need for a closer relationship between educational theory, subjects and practice

At present, I would suggest that the relationship between academic and professional studies is extremely tenuous. Yet, if the logical and psychological aspects of learning and teaching are at the core of the work in a college, a very close link must be established between subject and education departments, as well as between schools and colleges. It would probably be generally accepted that the good teacher is one who knows his pupils, who has a sound grasp of the subjects he teaches, and an understanding of a range of methods most likely to facilitate the learning of concepts, principles, facts, skills and attitudes at the different stages of children's conceptual development. He will also know how to motivate children and to evaluate whether meaningful learning has been achieved. What does this imply for students? It means that for each area of the school curriculum that they are likely to teach, they must know what children should learn, why some concepts are more fundamental than others, when they should learn and how they learn. The responsibility for building up this knowledge and expertise lies with the theory and practice of education and also with the curriculum courses. These components of the college programme should be designed to exemplify the conceptual interconnections between educational theory and the nature of different subjects, as well as demonstrating how this knowledge can impinge on educational practice. At the moment many college courses fail to draw out these crucial relationships. For instance, the educational theory may be arid and divorced from realistic practice; the psychological development of children may be studied without examining the nature of the content that is to be learnt; the relationship between how children learn and the structure of knowledge may not be explored; suggested teaching methods may be unrealistic; and if interdisciplinary approaches are in fact discussed, very little attempt may be made to spell out the inherent complex conceptual relationships.

This situation ought to improve. The link between schools and colleges during initial training and the probationary year needs to be strengthened, whilst the colleges themselves could establish a system of joint planning and team teaching between subject and education lecturers for the first, middle and secondary age ranges. In this way an attempt could be made to examine the logical and psychological aspects of learning and teaching a subject, as well as providing a sound grounding in content and method. Four components, involving a subject specialist, a philosopher, a psychologist and an experienced teacher, seem to be essential in such a course, which would include:

1. *Subject*
(a) The nature of the discipline.
 (i) Basic factual knowledge of selected areas of study.
 (ii) Central concepts and fundamental ideas of the discipline.
(iii) Methods of inquiry and validation procedures.

(b) The relationship between the subject and other areas of knowledge.

(c) The justification for including the subject in the school curriculum.

(d) The aims of teaching the subject in school.

(e) Appropriate subject-matter for different age groups.

(f) The criteria that can be used for determining the selection of subject-matter.

(g) Teaching methods and classroom activities.

(h) Audio-visual material.

2. *Philosophy*

(a) The nature and structure of knowledge.

(b) Educational justifications.

(c) Curriculum objectives.

(d) Criteria for the selection of subject-matter.

(e) The logical connection between 'learning' and 'teaching'.

(f) Concept formation.

(g) Interdisciplinary relationships.

3. *Psychology*

(a) The psychological development of children.

(b) The learning of different types of content (e.g. facts, skills, concepts).

(c) Motivational factors in learning.

(d) Educational technology.

(e) Evaluation procedures and testing.

4. *Teachers*

(a) Teaching methods.

(b) Children's learning.

(c) Motivation.

(d) Management techniques.

(e) Organizational problems.

(f) Record keeping.

This scheme has some theoretical advantages, but without meticulous planning, coordination and cooperative teaching it could present many major organizational hazards which would result in conceptual confusion on the part of the students. Joint teaching may not always be feasible, but it is of paramount importance that the initial *planning* of such courses is a combined operation, centred on a detailed blueprint of the education course. With this in mind, a stronge case could be made for each college to have an academic vice-principal whose central task would be to act as curriculum coordinator. If no positive effort is made to draw out the conceptual and practical relationships between educational theory subjects and practice at the planning stage, it is unlikely that links will be established during the teaching of these courses. Yet it is this knowledge of concepts, structures, validation procedures and the ability to grasp interconnections that lies at the heart of 'professionalism'. Perhaps it is little wonder that teaching is often regarded as a low-status profession, because its underlying theory and knowledge are still comparatively underdeveloped, and the knowledge that does exist is not always understood or put into practice.

The need for greater differentiation in the education and training of student teachers

Earlier in this chapter I questioned whether it is possible for a college to produce 'a teacher' who by virtue of his initial training would be really competent to teach in any sort of school. Or rather, has the time come for us to consider seriously the concept of a rationally based differentiated profession in which the student is trained to carry out a specific specialized function? In fact, should there be programme differentiation over the amount and area of subject-matter specialization depending on the age of pupils to be taught? The two programmes examined in this section apply especially to colleges of education as constituted at present. This sort of concurrent education and training is most relevant to those students with a reasonably firm commitment to teaching before entering college. A variety of different types of courses will be discussed in the penultimate section of this chapter.

First-school programme. In the first school (i.e. five to eight/nine age group) the present pattern of one teacher, largely responsible for all the activities of a particular class, is likely to continue. If so, it does seem rather incongruous that teachers who should be able to understand the concepts, structure and validation procedures of several areas of knowledge are still given an academic education in one traditionally designed main subject. The structure of courses for students in this category must be influenced partly by the distinctive nature of the first school. If a teacher is expected to have a specialist's understanding of young children, together with expertise in how to teach basic skills and a wide range of subjects, the college curriculum must reflect these professional and academic demands. For instance, in his inaugural lecture Professor Hollins points out that 'the curriculum of an infants' class is flexible and diffuse, with the child rather than the subject-matter in the forefront, in a family relationship with the class teacher'[18]. He doubts the relevance of the main academic subject to the education of teachers of young children and he argues for considerable differentiation in training. Professor Conant also suggests that first-school student teachers should be prepared in the content and methodology of all the subjects likely to be encountered in school. He considers that a broader academic programme is relevant and that study in depth in a single subject is unnecessary[19]. This view has been echoed by Professor Peters, who has suggested that teachers of younger children ought to have a 'liberal education in the main areas of the primary curriculum – science, mathematics, English, social studies and one of the arts – instead of doing a main subject, together with a thorough knowledge of how to teach these subjects at the appropriate level'[20].

There are several disadvantages in giving these students a more general education. For instance, a badly conceived programme could contain a large variety of superficial survey courses. Students might fail to gain an understanding of the different disciplines; they might be unable to identify key terms and handle the procedural skills; and they might never grasp the principles underlying each activity. Courses liable to degenerate into this sort of low-level awareness of *what* one knows, instead of a fundamental understanding of *how* one knows, could quite justifiably be branded as 'intellectual tourism'[21] or a 'smorgasbord academic programme'[22]. Nevertheless, such superficiality is not an inevitable result of a general education, which can be exacting if students are encouraged to master the appropriate methods of inquiry and to understand the distinctive qualities of each area of knowledge. In fact, the idea of 'academic study' must be applied to a programme of general education.

Dropping the main subject could also be criticized on other grounds. For example, it could present recruitment problems, as a more general course might not attract those sixth-form students who wish to read one subject at a higher level. In addition, the B.Ed. degree could present a major obstacle to change as it is focused on the study of the main subject and of education. But is the present concept of a first degree sacrosanct? Traditional university thinking permeates the structure of many academic courses in colleges, but is this model ideal for an institution which differs from universities both in function and character [23]? The teachers' unions could object to a differentiation in initial training on the grounds that it might create a hierarchical structure within the profession, thereby jeopardizing the status of the first-school teacher and reducing mobility within the teaching force. But I don't think these consequences necessarily follow. Although immediately after college a teacher would be less mobile than at present, this would be compensated for by having a body of teachers more highly skilled to carry out a specific function. This would strengthen the claim for a knowledge-based, rationally constituted profession, in which a strong sense of unity would be achieved through diversity of function. We are likely to see a coherent system of in-service 'adjustment' courses established to facilitate flexibility. Initial training will be regarded only as a preliminary preparation for teaching, and systematic retraining will operate in relation to specialized professional functions, thus enabling teachers to attain higher academic and educational qualifications. The supposed disadvantages do not invalidate the provision of a rationally determined programme of general education for first-school students, which could be both academically demanding and professionally relevant.

Middle-school programme. The middle school of the future presents a range of different problems for the college curriculum, mainly because it will require more specialist teaching than is offered in most present primary schools [24]. This is not to advocate formal traditional subject teaching in middle schools, but to reflect the growing demands on teachers from team teaching and the new curriculum development projects. Apart from the first transitional year in a middle school, when it may be still more appropriate for one teacher to be largely responsible for the activities and work of a particular class, teachers will have to do some specialist teaching in several areas of the curriculum, as well as acting as subject advisers to teams of teachers. In the words of the *Plowden Report*, a middle school

... with semi-specialist accommodation shared between cognate subjects, and teachers skilled in certain areas of the curriculum rather than in single subjects, could provide a bridge from class teaching to specialization, and from investigation of general problems to subject disciplines[25].

This view would be shared by Professor Conant, for he suggests that the programme for middle-school student teachers 'should provide depth of content and methods of teaching in a specific subject or cluster of subjects' normally taught to this age group (i.e. eight/nine to twelve/thirteen years of age)[26]. If middle-school teachers are not to be expected to teach more than three or four subjects, the present multiplicity of curriculum courses seems unnecessary, and more time and resources should be devoted to giving the students a thorough knowledge of both the children and the subjects that they intend to teach.

The basic structure of a programme for these students could comprise one core (or main) subject, supported by two or three related contextual subjects, which would be designed to set the different disciplines in their cognitive frame and to draw out possible conceptual relationships[27]. A variety of combinations could be offered, including:

Language	– English literature and drama, movement
Movement	– language, art, drama
Art	– movement, music, social history
History	– English literature, art, history of ideas
Divinity	– history, history of ideas, English literature
Geography	– history, science, sociology (i.e. environmental studies)
Mathematics	– science, geography
Science	– mathematics, history of ideas

But if the main subject is retained for middle-school student teachers, its present structure must be questioned. The study of an area of knowledge for intrinsic reasons *alone* is not a distinguishing feature of a college of education, for all academic studies can be conducted within a framework of professional relevance. This view has implications not only for the actual structure of the main course, but also for the sort of subject selected for study and the approaches to teaching it. Perhaps some middle-school students would find main courses in children's language development or the sequential learning of mathematics, for instance, both academically exacting and professionally highly valuable.

Although most colleges of education are likely to concentrate on training first- and middle-school teachers, those offering secondary courses could consider new areas of study such as mathematics and philosophy, sociology and philosophy, environmental sciences or European studies, which would help to meet the need of new courses being introduced into the more enlightened secondary schools.

In all such cases I would suggest that each core and contextual subject should comprise four inter-related elements:

1. The nature of the discipline. (Ideally, subject-matter should be selected to exemplify the main features and procedural skills of the discipline, as well as satisfying the criterion of professional relevance.)

2. The place of the subject in education (e.g. aims and justifications).

3. The psychological aspects of learning the subject.

4. Subject-matter for schools and teaching methods.

These four components seem to be of crucial importance in the structure of the core and contextual subjects for middle-school student teachers. They allow students to engage in academic study of some rigour without sacrificing the idea of professional relevance. In fact, the interaction between academic and professional studies is central to such a course, in the hope that disciplined theoretical study will impinge on educational practice. This sort of programme would require joint planning and some team teaching, thereby strengthening communication between subject and education departments, and between schools and colleges.

New directions for the curriculum

The central aim of any teacher education programme must be to raise the professional and academic standards of the teacher, thereby enhancing his status in society and meeting the needs of future generations of children. There is no one solution: we must allow for different structures, new initiatives and flexibility both within and between a range of institutions. Individual colleges must be encouraged to strike out on their own and to develop curricula which satisfy certain agreed public standards, but which are not restricted by conservative traditions. One of the first moves could be to break the present near monopoly of teacher education by the universities and colleges of education, and offer a broader-based supply of teachers, with the Council for National Academic Awards playing a more active role in the planning of courses and in the examination of students. Teacher education need not be limited to any one institution, for it could be developed in universities, polytechnics, colleges of technology and colleges of art as well as in colleges of education. It is significant to notice the new policy statement of the ATCDE which supports 'the concept of a federated group of colleges in association with a parent university'[28].

A strong case can be made for training some student teachers in multi-vocational institutions, with the intention of trying to break the current academic and social isolation. As early as 1924 Lance Jones, in his large-scale analysis of teacher training, suggested that 'the intending teacher should be associated as long and as fully as possible with students preparing for other walks of life'[29]. The Robbins Committee, although recognizing the aspiration of the colleges of education to integrate more closely with the universities, also appreciated the value of a move towards a more multi-vocational type of college. It recommended 'experiments with institutions that bridge the traditional gap between colleges for the education of teachers and institutions of further education which prepare their students for other professions'[30]. Again, Edward Britton, the

General Secretary of the NUT, has questioned why teachers should be singled out to be trained in a specialist institution. He has commented that:

There is a good case to be made for the normal teacher training to take place at the technical college rather than in a specialist institution. . . . It is difficult to see what there is about teaching that makes the segregation of the student teacher necessary. Teachers would gain academically, socially and in the breadth of their intellectual experience if they were trained with other people entering other professions[31].

This view could be challenged on the grounds that an initial common course for teachers, related welfare fields and quite different occupations is inappropriate and impractical, and that students would not necessarily widen their intellectual horizons in such an environment. As early as 1933, when R. W. Rich was discussing the merits of the relationship between universities and day training colleges, he observed that:

Because of the demands of the professional part of the course, there was often a considerable segregation of the education students from the other students of the college, so that one of the alleged benefits of the day training college, that of mixing teachers in training with men and women preparing for professions, was lost[32].

The point to emphasize, however, is that if teachers could gain professionally and educationally by receiving part of their training alongside students entering other occupations, the curriculum must be planned to allow for common optional subjects, for instance, within an initial foundation year. The consecutive 'end-on' type of course (discussed below; see schemes A and B) might defer the more specifically professional dimension of the student's training, but it would benefit the young student who has not committed himself to any particular occupation at the age of eighteen. Furthermore, if joint courses for teachers, social workers, probationary officers and youth leaders were established, this would allow for greater mobility between allied professions and would avoid making the student teacher feel that he is entering a 'captive' profession.

The training of non-graduate teachers

Possible new approaches for the initial training of non-graduate teachers in a multi-vocational college could include:

Scheme A. Year 1: A common academic foundation year in a range of optional subjects, some of which could be grouped in interdisciplinary areas. The aim would be to develop an understanding of the central facts, concepts, structures and verification procedures of each area of knowledge studied, and to draw out possible cognitive relationships.

Year 2: Students could opt for a particular professional area and a joint course could be established for potential teachers and the related welfare fields. The academic component would continue from the first year, but the curriculum would begin to have a more professional orientation, introducing educational theory and practice.

Years 3 and 4: A distinctive curriculum could now be provided for each occupational group. The academic element in the teacher programme would be retained, but it would be conceived strictly within a professional frame of reference.

Scheme B. A two-year academic foundation programme could be established, with students opting at the end of this period for a further two years of professional education related to their specific occupation. Again this could be attractive to the student who wants to keep his options open and to delay his choice of career.

Scheme C. For those students committed to the idea of teaching, the present system of three years' concurrent initial training together with a probationary year is appropriate. Nevertheless, the actual structure of the curriculum should be fundamentally altered on the lines discussed previously, allowing for programme differentation and a close interaction between academic and professional studies. This sort of teacher-education curriculum could be implemented in either a college of education or a multi-vocational institution; it need not be restricted to a mono-professional setting.

Scheme D. A further scheme could operate in a variety of institutions, whereby the less academic student teacher could undergo a two-year course of professional education leading to a Part I of the Teacher's Certificate, thus enabling him to become a teacher assistant. This initial qualification could be converted into a full Teacher's Certificate by either returning to college for a year of full-time study, or by preparing for the Part II part time. As in all the other schemes, this sandwich approach could still lead on to a full- or part-time B.Ed. course, if the appropriate standards were satisfied.

The training of graduate teachers

This area of initial training, whereby graduates experience one year's professional study in either a college or university department of education, has been subjected to a barrage of criticism in recent years. By and large its present curriculum comprises method courses, educational theory, and up to about ten weeks of school experience. But how can one year be considered an adequate preparation for a profession as complex as teaching? Presumably the principles underlying a teacher-education curriculum, as conceived in this chapter, apply equally to graduate-teacher programmes.

In his degree course a student should have engaged in the objective study of an area of knowledge, and pursued it in depth for intrinsic reasons. Through this academic study he ought to have learnt to ask certain sorts of questions such as: What are the fundamental concepts of the discipline and how are they related to create a distinctive style of thinking? What does it mean 'to know' in the particular mode of thought and what methods of inquiry are used to evaluate the truth of statements? In other words, a degree course should enable a student to reflect critically on the logic and nature of his discipline and to view its unique characteristics in relation to the wider spectrum of knowledge. But even if a graduate has reached this stage of precision, mastery and critical reflection, it doesn't necessarily follow that he can become a competent teacher through one year of training. Throughout this chapter it has been maintained that the logical and psychological aspects of learning and teaching a subject lie at the heart of a teacher education curriculum. Therefore, the graduate student teacher must study a wide area of educational theory before he can grasp the relationships between this knowledge, his subject and educational practice. It would seem that if the consecutive course for training graduates is to continue, it must be extended to *two* years of professional education, including at least two terms of school experience. For instance, much of the second year could act as a period of school-based training instead of the present probationary year. If we are to achieve a knowledge-based profession, a period of two years' preparation for teaching is the bare minimum we can allow, despite financial pressures to limit the length of training.

But perhaps we ought to start looking seriously at some of the newer universities which have established concurrent combined degree courses in one or more subjects together with education as a principal or subsidiary component. At present about fourteen universities run such courses, including Aberystwyth, Bangor, Bath, Bradford, Brunel, Cardiff, Keele, Lancaster, Salford, Stirling, Sussex, Swansea, Ulster and York. A range of possibilities opens up with the concept of a combined degree. For instance:

1. A three-year concurrent course in one main subject and education followed by a one-year Graduate Certificate in Education, in which two terms of teaching practice is feasible, as at the University of York.

2. A one-year foundation course for *all* students, as at Keele, followed by a three-year combined degree in either (a) two main subjects, one of which being educational theory and practice, and two subsidiary subjects, or (b) one main subject and education, including professional training and practice.

3. A four-year combined degree in one main subject and education, in which academic and professional studies run concurrently throughout the course.

Numerous advantages accrue from this sort of combined degree course. First, it allows academic and professional study to be closely inter-related, thereby achieving a high level of conceptual sophistication within a professional frame of reference. It also enables educational practice to be an integral feature of the whole course, with the result that a longer period may be spent in schools than with the more conventional

Graduate Certificate course. Moreover, important links can be effected in a number of distinct ways – for instance, between education tutors and subject lecturers in the combining faculties; between academic and professional studies; between theory and practice; and between universities and schools, especially if a teacher-tutor system operates, whereby certain teachers become explicitly involved in the professional training of students.

Postscript

This chapter has been devoted largely to the initial training of student teachers, but this is not to ignore the importance of in-service education for experienced teachers. The three-year college course, for instance, can be expected to act only as an introduction to the most professionally relevant aspects of education, thus developing sufficient theoretically based technical skills to enable a teacher to operate competently in his first post. Ideally, those courses designed for the education of the students should be able to build on sound foundations laid at school, but this is not always the case in practice. Colleges of education should not have to make all students attend a wide range of basic content or survey courses; this is hardly the function of higher education. Courses must be structured to draw out *how* one knows, as well as *what* one knows; the emphasis must be more on the conceptualization, explanation and verification of knowledge in a discipline, rather than on the learning of inert information. Admittedly, there is a limit to how far a student can take such academic study in the time available, but programmes must be planned to draw out the essential thinking of the subjects to be taught, so that a new teacher can move around with confidence and understanding within each area of knowledge.

But initial training can hardly be expected to develop in students a *mastery* of that specialized theoretical and practical knowledge which is necessary if teachers are to gain the authority, autonomy and understanding fundamental to the making of rational professional judgements. Teachers need to engage in continual professional education if they are to perform their multifarious roles, many of which are subject to constant redefinition due to changing social, technological and educational demands. It is only armed with this new knowledge and technical expertise that teachers can give their children a worth-while education. Furthermore, it would enable all members of the profession to participate more effectively in the making of policy decisions on such central issues as the structure and content of the curriculum, teaching methods, school organization and teacher education.

In recent years there has been a growing recognition of the importance of in-service training, as can be seen from the wide variety of courses and activities being offered by university Institutes and departments of education, polytechnics, colleges of education, the Department of Education and Science, local education authorities (e.g. through teacher centres and county residential centres) and the subject associations[33]. The aim of this training is to improve the quality of teaching by strengthening the teacher's knowledge and understanding of the educational process. Sometimes this takes the form of post-initial degrees and advanced diplomas, but in general it involves teachers attending short courses or engaging in activities within their own locality. There is evidence to show that a large number of teachers want their in-service work to concentrate on such practical problems as teaching methods, aids and materials, and the development of new teaching schemes and programmes[34]. But how far should courses be designed to meet only these short-term objectives, however important in themselves? In fact, how can teachers be expected to devise new curricula without extending their knowledge of educational theory and the structure of particular disciplines? This implies that they need to keep abreast of the expansion of knowledge itself, as well as with recent developments in teaching methodology. Opportunities must be given for teachers to discuss the possible application of recent research findings to work in schools.

But in-service education must be more comprehensive than this. If the teaching force is to become more differentiated in character, systematic retraining will have to be established in relation to a wide range of specialized professional functions. Moreover, as schools become more involved with the preparation of students (perhaps through the 'teacher-tutor' system), the teachers concerned will need special training in order to perform their additional role. This will enable them to reflect critically on the nature of teaching and to examine the principles underlying the activities that ought to take place in a classroom. Another category of training is required for head-teachers, deputy heads and heads of departments, all of whom need to be skilled in organization and management, as well as having a wide conceptual grasp of educational policy and curriculum planning. Finally, as the pressure for an all-graduate profession mounts, provision must be made for those teachers who are qualified and who wish to read for a degree in education.

This shifting focus towards in-service education is vital if we are to achieve a scientifically based profession. There is an urgent need to make explicit the relationship between initial and further training, and also to examine the objectives, organization and coordination of all in-service programmes. Such an examination must rest on the premise that schools, teacher centres, colleges and universities ought to be in a coherent system, whereby initial training, the probationary year and in-service education form a continuum based on a body of rationally determined principles.

Some of the suggestions in this chapter for the reform of the teacher education curriculum have been recognized by a few colleges and universities, and Area Training Organizations are being asked to reappraise existing structures and courses. Perhaps some independent national body, such as a colleges council, needs to be established in order to coordinate developments in teacher education. But whatever course is pursued in the future, constructive curriculum reform can only come from the active participation of all elements of the profession.

References

1. For statistics see *The Times Educational Supplement*, 13 February 1970, p. 73.
2. Standing Conference of Area Training Organizations, *Summary of Proposed Courses in Training Colleges*, February 1949, paras. 2 a–c.

3. For instance, see J. Kay-Shuttleworth, *Four Periods of Public Education*, London, 1862, pp. 338–53.

4. University of London Institute of Education, *Regulations and Syllabuses for the Teacher's Certificate*, 1951–2, para. 8, pp. 7–8.

5. *Fifth Report of the National Advisory Council on the Training and Supply of Teachers: Three-Year Training and Teachers*, HMSO, 1956; *Sixth Report of the National Advisory Council on the Training and Supply of Teachers: Scope and Content of the Three-Year Course of Teacher Training*, HMSO, 1957.

6. Ministry of Education, *The Training of Teachers*, pamphlet no. 34, HMSO, 1957.

7. For instance, see *Newcastle Commission General Report*, vol. 1, 1862, p. 132; L. G. E. Jones, *The Training of Teachers in England and Wales*, Oxford University Press, 1924, p. 87; *Teachers and Youth Leaders (McNair Report)*, HMSO, 1944, para. 204, p. 65.

8. Committee on Higher Education, *Higher Education (Robbins Report)*, HMSO, 1963, para. 341, p. 116.

9. P. H. Hirst, 'Educational theory', in J. W. Tibble (ed.), *The Study of Education*, Routledge & Kegan Paul, 1966, ch. 2.

10. For instance, see P. Renshaw, 'A reappraisal of the college of education curriculum', *Education for Teaching*, vol. 75, 1968, pp. 28–34; H. Rée, 'Wanted – a Royal Commission', *Higher Education Review*, vol. 1, 1968, pp. 55–62; T. H. B. Hollins, *Another Look at Teacher Training*, Leeds University Press, 1969; Sub-Committee of the National Young Teacher Advisory Council of the NUT, *The Future of Teacher Education*, 1968; NUT, 'Teacher education – the way ahead', discussion document, 1970; National Foundation for Educational Research, *Teacher Training*, memorandum submitted to the Parliamentary Select Committee on Education, 1970; letter from the Secretary of State for Education and Science to Area Training Organizations, 19 February 1970.

11. J. Bray, *Decision in Government*, Gollancz, 1970, pp. 96–103.

12. NUT, 'Teacher education – the way ahead', discussion document, 1970, paras. 41–3, p. 16.

13. W. Taylor, *Society and the Education of Teachers*, Faber, 1969, pp. 56–8.

14. P. Renshaw, 'A concept of a college of education', M. Phil. thesis, University of London, 1969, sect. 2, ch. 6.

15. Central Advisory Council for Education (England), *Children and their Primary Schools* (*Plowden Report*), HMSO, 1967, para. 406, p. 151.

16. P. H. Hirst, 'Liberal education and the nature of knowledge', in R. D. Archambault (ed.), *Philosophical Analysis and Education*, Routledge & Kegan Paul, 1965, pp. 116–21.

17. See J. Higginbotham, 'The concepts of professional and academic studies in relation to courses in institutes of higher education (particularly colleges of education)', *British Journal of Educational Studies*, vol. 17, no. 1, 1969, pp. 54–65.

18. T. H. B. Hollins, *Another Look at Teacher Training*, Leeds University Press, 1969, p. 9.

19. J. B. Conant, *The Education of American Teachers*, McGraw-Hill, 1963, p. 155.

20. R. S. Peters, 'Education as a specific preparation for teaching', in *Proceedings of the Conference on the Education and Training of Teachers*, Department of Education and Science, 1967, p. 4.

21. D. Bell, *The Reforming of General Education*, Columbia University Press, 1966, p. 227.

22. M. Lieberman, 'Why liberal education does not liberalise', in M. Lieberman (ed.), *The Future of Public Education*, University of Chicago Press, 1960, p. 151.

23. J. W. Tibble (ed.), *The Study of Education*, Routledge & Kegan Paul, 1966, p. 231.

24. Central Advisory Council for Education (England), *Children and their Primary Schools* (*Plowden Report*), HMSO, 1967, paras. 382–3, pp. 145–6.

25. Central Advisory Council for Education (England), *Children and their Primary Schools* (*Plowden Report*), HMSO, 1967, para. 381, p. 145.

26. J. B. Conant, *The Education of American Teachers*, McGraw-Hill, 1963, p. 155.

27. A. Briggs, 'Drawing a new map of learning', in D. Daiches (ed.), *The Idea of a New University*, Deutsch, 1964, pp. 62–4.

28. ATCDE, *Higher Education and Preparation for Teaching: A Policy for Colleges of Education*, 1970, para. 6.0, p. 4.

29. L. G. E. Jones, *The Training of Teachers in England and Wales*, Oxford University Press, 1924, p. 388.

30. Committee on Higher Education, *Higher Education (Robbins Report)*, HMSO, 1963, para. 489, p. 159.

31. E. Britton, 'The teaching profession and the education of teachers', in *Towards a Policy for the Education of Teachers*, Colston Research Society, Bristol, 1968, p. 16.

32. R. W. Rich, *The Training of Teachers in England and Wales during the Nineteenth Century*, Cambridge University Press, 1933, p. 229.

33. D. J. Johnston, 'In-service evolution', *Education for Teaching*, vol. 80, 1969, pp. 4–10.

34. B. Cane, *In-Service Training*, National Foundation for Educational Research, 1969, p. 23.

Part Three
New Structures

5 The Teaching Profession and the Training of Teachers
Margaret Maden

It is often assumed that arguments concerning the training of teachers are centred on the need to improve the schools. However, if this is true for students, Parliamentary Select Committees and education correspondents, it is not always true for the teachers. The teaching profession is concerned with protecting and extending its own status as well as with promoting educational change. It hopes, of course, that the needs of status and education will converge, but contradictions between them often occur, sometimes needlessly, sometimes irreconcilably. There are also issues, like the policy for vastly increasing the numbers in teacher training, where the profession will insist on educational objectives (more teachers) being paramount and will virtually refuse to examine the policy's implications either for themselves or for the schools.

The teaching profession has no one organization representing itself, and in most cases reference to the National Union of Teachers is most appropriate for evidence of professional attitudes. The NUT is the largest single body for teachers in all types of schools and it is also the organization without whose agreement no real structural change in either the schools or the profession can take place. The NUT can act in an enlightened and radical way, as in its evidence to the Plowden Committee and the Public Schools Commission, or it can act in a more restrictive way, as over parental help in schools or in anything relating to the organization, role and work of the teachers. The NUT embodies within itself all the contradictions of the teaching profession at large – what's good for the children isn't necessarily good for the teachers. Genuine concern for children and for the State system of education are important features in policy making within the union, but the NUT is also financed to protect and extend the rights of its members. That the rights and aspirations of both teachers and children coincide fairly frequently is fortunate but, in the teacher training issue at least, not inevitable. For example, if Peter Renshaw's arguments in chapter 4 are at all correct in pressing for more specialist groups of teachers from first school onwards, then the teaching profession must reconsider one of its major beliefs concerning the nature of the 'good teacher'. In the NUT's initial discussion document on teacher training[1] the concept of the good teacher is listed as follows:

One who can adapt himself to the changing nature and needs of children in varying age ranges, in depressing or congenial surroundings, and who can, in any one of these situations, satisfy the needs and demands of the differing children who make up each class. The teacher, in order to cope with a possible variety of teaching situations, will, as part of his professional expertise, need to understand the distinctive concepts, structure and validity in the disciplines that fall under educational theory and in those subjects or subject areas that he is likely to teach.

Anyone who has come to understand the structure and concepts of a single discipline may understandably query the validity of asking a teacher to master the same for several disciplines in a three-year course.

This prescription for the good teacher is along the lines of most existing teacher training courses in colleges of education, and implies that training should be directed towards the general teacher. Arguments that such objectives are over-diffuse and conceptually unworkable are, however, irrelevant in terms of the NUT's real reasons for such a goal. Later on, in the same document, more critical arguments are reached.

One of the strengths of the teaching profession in England and Wales has for many years been the general principle of single qualification which did not, by implication, result in primary and secondary teaching being considered mutually exclusive. In recent years some educationalists, both within and without the teaching profession, have called for a teaching profession in which there is a hierarchical structure ... the Union cannot endorse any structural change in initial training that would tend towards teacher immobility.

This argument reveals two unwarranted assumptions: first, that specialist training for different sectors of the school system is necessarily hierarchical and, second, that career immobility is associated with patterns of training. But if the profession and Union really want complete mobility and a non-hierarchical structure, then the controlling factors lie as much if not more within the salary structure and 'points system' as with the training. The NUT also asks for a lengthening of the present three-year basic Certificate course to four years, leading, it hopes, to an all-graduate profession. The Union, and the profession at large, has to decide whether it wishes to develop its status by simply lengthening a general teacher training course to four years, or by more radical means. The profession could, for example, state clearly that the work of different groups of teachers is so complex and specialized that not only are adequate salaries required, but also carefully designed courses for the preparation of such teachers. It is surely beginning to be clear that the infant-school teacher should possess special skills and knowledge of, for example, child development and psychology relevant to that age group and that these skills and knowledge are different from those needed by the teacher of adolescents in a comprehensive school. It would seem also to make more political sense for the teachers' major union to use this as a status and salary bargaining point, rather than to regard the all-round general teacher as inseparable from the maintenance or extension of status. In fact, ordinary rank-and-file members of the Union often confess their own incompetence. Clearly, this cannot be admitted publicly by the NUT, but the schizophrenia between teachers' privately acknowledged inadequacies (for example, the increasing desperation felt by many traditionally trained teachers faced with the demands of mixed-ability group teaching in comprehensive schools) and the public 'stand-together' at the national level is both absurd and self-defeating. Answers to both the question of teachers, through no fault of their own, becoming outdated, and the question of career immobility, lie not in monolithic schemes for initial training, but rather in a massive investment in in-service training. The Union should be pressing hard for statutory in-service retraining for those teachers who wish, mid-career, to change or develop their initial area of specialism. This is a useful example of how fear of lowered status (in primary-school teachers in particular) inhibits proper consideration of either educational improvements or of the real determinants of status.

Status considerations seem to over-ride even the educational considerations most sharply felt by individual teachers. It is frequently assumed in national NUT debates that higher teacher status will, of itself, ensure better learning procedures in schools. Whilst it is clearly desirable and necessary that the major teachers' unions should concern themselves with the universities, the DES and the Council for National Academic Awards, it is none the less regrettable that more policy does not emerge directly from some of the more traumatic experiences of teachers in schools. For example, in local association meetings of teachers, outside London, there is scant interest shown in the great power struggles between the university senates, the DES and other national 'goliaths'. The major grievances are associated with the contacts between existing college and department staff and teachers in schools. Alarming stories invariably emerge concerning frightened, inadequate and apologetic college lecturers unable to 'save' rampaging classes. Tales of ill-prepared and ill-motivated students follow one after the other with increasing evidence of ineptitude. Teachers' favourite stories inevitably relate to their worst-favoured and ill-equipped colleagues leaving for a 'rest cure' (i.e. a lecturing job in a college of education). Sadly there is often some truth in such stories, but the interpretation of such symptoms – for that is what such stories represent – is almost always lacking. The Unions, at national level, should use such anxieties and frustrations from their own teacher members for a close and detailed attack on present teacher education. For example, the inadequate college tutor entering a school in which he has no more skill and expertise to offer than the student he is 'supervising', simply expresses the fact that colleges employ subject specialists and then actually use them for some quite unrelated function. The ill-prepared-student phenomenon should again be examined from the standpoint of college courses straddling a watered-down academicism and an educational theory unrelated to the rigours and changing curricula of schools. The action which should follow from such critical analyses includes, for example, the introduction of teacher-tutors and other means of developing firm relationships in what Dr Edith Cope of the Bristol Institute has described as the 'triangle of the college tutor, student and teacher'. The teaching profession itself should take this triangle situation and negotiate a good allowance for such liaison positions through Burnham. The NUT's latest teacher-education proposals do, in fact, recommend such developments. There should also be someone in each school who, apart from advising students, should act as a link-man between the theories and objectives of the teacher-educators and the realities and constraints of the school itself. The teaching profession itself, in other words, should increasingly participate in the training process and new initiatives should emerge from teachers. The links between school and college would be a two-way process. The anti-intellectualism and resistance to theory so often encountered in schools on the part of teachers should also be ameliorated with firmer, more structured contacts. The NUT should use its political weight not just for recommending monolithic initial courses and structures of teacher training in higher education, but for creating procedures at the most sensitive point of experience for most teachers, namely, the schools themselves.

Probably the major ambivalence in the profession's attitude to the training of teachers concerns supply and quality. The teacher's professional associations all agree on the need for a vastly increased supply of teachers. The NUT gains as much support from its own ranks on class sizes as it does on salaries. The NUT and other teacher associations agree that to reduce primary-school classes to thirty-five, and secondary classes to thirty, would mean 40,000 more teachers. Their supply is always seen in terms of increasing the entry to the colleges of education, which produce some 80 per cent of our teachers – the remaining 20 per cent coming from the less controllable university sector. At the same time as they demand this, however, the unions all want much higher entry qualifications. Evidence from the Central Registry and Clearing House suggests that numbers of students entering colleges of education with two advanced level subjects has remained, during the 1960s, at about

38 per cent. But about 25 per cent of college entrants have had no sixth-form, or equivalent, background.

The teachers are not alone in being ambivalent on this point. If we have no clear indication of the precise intellectual and social qualities needed to make a successful teacher, it is hard to be firm in asserting who should or should not be accepted into teacher training. It is well known that there is little correlation between A-level results and teaching performance. However, until more sophisticated entry conditions and assessment procedures are devised, colleges and teachers are likely to measure entry standards in the same way as the universities, namely by A-levels. The NUT Conference of 1970 rejected an executive call to maintain basic entry requirements as five O-levels and insisted that there should be more concentration on A-level standards. Unfortunately, as with most conference resolutions, it was left to officials in the NUT, DES and the Area Training Organizations to spell out the implications of the demand. It is unlikely that students with two or three A-level passes will take much note of NUT Conference resolutions. Bright sixth formers will continue to try for university, and on failing to gain a place will look elsewhere for their higher education. The colleges of education may not necessarily be next in their list, but rather the polytechnics and colleges of technology where there are ample degree opportunities. The colleges of education, in contrast, offer a mere 5 per cent of their students B.Ed. degree courses; it is hoped this will rise to 25 per cent by the mid-1970s.

Reduced to simple terms, the profession recognizes the low calibre of many entrants to colleges of education and sees that any substantial increase in their numbers will, under present circumstances, worsen it. There is no easy solution, but the NUT seems to have a two-fold remedy in the longer term. First, it recommends dramatic action by the Government on teachers' salaries and career prospects. The profession, it argues reasonably enough, cannot exist and prosper on a sense of vocationalism alone. Second, it recommends a phasing-out of the colleges of education, at least in their present form. The colleges, as monotechnics, possess an inbuilt disadvantage at student entry because a choice, or rather non-choice, of teaching as a career has to be made at too early an age. This 'trapping' effect, it is argued, depresses most bright sixth formers, who primarily seek a more open form of higher education before vocational commitment. However, there are significant numbers within the profession who still value the colleges of education system for its historic supply origins. In the NUT journal the *Teacher*, a a typical spokesman for this approach wrote, on 15 May 1970, of students: 'only a minority, apparently, are devoted to the idea of teaching. The professional moral of this is to recruit to the colleges only mature-age students who *want* to teach. Given this aim, how are we going to meet the raw needs of the schools for recruits sufficient in number to maintain, let alone reduce, the ratio of pupils to teachers?' The logic of this is to accept the present position and forget about improving quality, however quality is defined. However, what has to be questioned is the sufficiency of the NUT's two-fold remedy for supply and quality. Educationally and professionally it is based on the idea that in the next twenty years there should be around half a million teachers in schools all of similar status and qualification; further, that the qualification should be of degree level and undifferentiated. Maybe the NUT will succeed in pressurizing Governments to implement this, but it poses problems which do not appear to have been seriously examined by the NUT, or the profession in general.

The call for an all-graduate profession is strongest in the NUT where there is the greatest concentration of college-trained teachers. The predominant concern of this group is the acquisition of the social and professional status denied them by the college certification system. Most teachers welcomed the introduction of the B.Ed. degree, following Robbins, as a means of moving towards an all-graduate profession. But sharp problems are being created in schools by the arrival of the first B.Ed. graduates in 1969. Teachers are worried about the career role of these graduates. Not only, it appears, are they not especially good teachers and are divorced from the reality of schools, but they are introducing yet another component into the career hierarchy. College-trained teachers are threatened by decreasing career opportunities. Comprehensive reorganization has meant fewer posts of responsibility and fewer headships, and such posts are increasingly likely to be given to graduates, either in arts, science or, now, education. Persistent demands, largely associated with anxiety over status, arise for in-service, part-time opportunity for degree study. The NUT welcomes the Open University, not because it offers new ideas in professional expertise and knowledge, but because it takes the pressure off members without degree status. However, the profession should not merely grab at either Open University or B.Ed. degrees. Rather, it should examine closely both the exact salary–career implications and the professional relevance of such degrees.

Here the introduction of the B.Ed. into existing irrational salary structures should at least be questioned. The profession should examine the possibility of regarding a graduate teacher, and more especially one with a B.Ed., as having a training appropriate to a specific salary level and function within a school. It could also examine future patterns of training for different levels of work in schools. The vexed question of training auxiliary teachers to work under fully qualified teachers has not been discussed in the NUT with anything less than charged emotion and shouts of 'dilution'. Certainly, without necessarily accepting the motives of the DES for suggesting a second level of teacher (the auxiliary), it might be worth investigating whether or not there are levels of function within a school system warranting the use of less well-qualified people. Considering the increasing complexity of schools and of the learning process itself, teachers need not only technical aids but also human aids. Laboratory technicians and school-meals helpers are accepted by the NUT as 'ancillaries', but the recent rejection of the foreign-language assistants as not being qualified teachers, with a resultant loss of employment for many of them, reveals confused professional attitudes. There is thus a refusal to accept a middle role for qualified persons, not necessarily qualified teachers, in schools. For example, one would imagine that a person with a two-year art training could be usefully employed in a primary school taking small art groups without necessarily being a fully qualified three- or four-year trained teacher. Similarly, the growing trend in comprehensive schools towards pupil-conducted social and environmental surveys could easily utilize people in the community for short courses under the guidance of a fully qualified teacher.

Also such teacher 'aides' could accompany pupils for outside survey work as well as making the necessary arrangements for community visits and exchanges. Teachers should become, amongst other things, operational managers and less the 'all-rounder' who sees his task essentially as being with his class each and every hour in a seven-hour day. Such increasing use of a 'second-level' teacher or school worker might be worth investigating from both educational as well as status stand-points. This might be better than assuming that an all-graduate profession can be spread amongst our schools on either present or improved staffing standards. Teacher education need not be conceived entirely in terms of an all-graduate profession at the cost of rejecting other options – like a two-year training for a second level of teacher. What is essential is that all levels of training including higher degrees for teachers, not specifically mentioned so far, should allow teachers to achieve qualification from the first to the highest. In this sort of context, skilled prac-tising teachers could be given extensive access to degree study, and the NUT could negotiate links between a properly designed B.Ed. and career status. But this implies that the profession itself must initiate its own job analysis so that levels of qualifi-cation and education are related to both school function and salary. At present a certificated teacher is paid less and has fewer career chances than a teacher who happens to be a gra-duate in textile engineering or ancient Greek.

The teaching profession, especially the NUT, is now ques-tioning the validity of the institutions in which most teachers are trained, recognizing that the monotechnic principle has an undesirable 'trapping' effect and that the certificate system is primarily a means for depressing teachers' salaries. The idea that a certificate, unlike a degree, is non-negotiable in the open market is now familiar, but strategy for the dissolution or broadening of the colleges is by no means agreed. The major problem for the NUT is its view, shared by the ATCDE, that the universities are vital and important in the present structure. The role of the universities in the development of the B.Ed. ought to have made the profession at least sceptical of their academic control, but NUT policy here remains essentially pre-Robbins. The Union stated in its 1970 discussion document:

> The spirit of the Union's proposal was accepted by the Robbins Committee, who proposed that the then training colleges should be grouped to form schools of education attached to a university in the area ... the experience of the last six years has in no way convinced the Union that the essence of its proposal as interpreted by the Robbins Committee was not both desirable and realistic.

The Robbins proposals make it clear that the colleges would still have precious little autonomy and that the final arbiter in development of courses, whether for the B.Ed. or not, would be the university:

> The degrees granted to the students in colleges of education would be degrees of the university, and in all arrangements that it made for them the school of education would be responsible to the university senate.

The NUT reasserts this Robbins policy even while at the same time calling for a complete reorganization of higher education with regional control and national coordination. The Union wants comprehensive universities, though the Robbins policies make this impossible under any reasonable interpretation of the term 'comprehensive'. This further ambivalence stems from the profession's desire for status and its belief that status is primarily associated with traditional universities, whether or not the universities continue to despise teacher education. For example, in replying to Shirley Williams's thirteen possibilities for reducing university cost, the vice-chancellors suggested that the colleges of education could take on more students at lower cost, to do, presumably, lower-level work within a revamped liberal arts colleges. That the vice-chancellors seek to solve their problems with the Government through the colleges of education is one thing. That the teaching profession actually agrees to such proposals and asks for the retention of a low-level association with the universities is another, and sadder, matter.

The profession's attitude to the universities is also revealed through the B.Ed. development. Rarely is there any intellectual or conceptual challenge to the B.Ed.'s structure and content. It is assumed that the degree, in its various forms, has faults in practical terms, but that its theoretical content is best left to the university boards of studies and senates. This acceptance of a dichotomy between the academic and the practical is the most dangerous aspect of the present B.Ed., for it means that B.Ed. graduates will offer little extra to the schools. It also means a permanent ceiling on numbers entering for it, operated on academic not professional criteria. The NUT policy reinforces the division by encouraging the universities to remain final arbiters in the development of degrees and other courses.

The NUT also supports the continuance of the Area Training Organizations which are housed in, and administered by, the university Institutes of Education. These Organizations have on their central committees representatives of the teachers' associations and local education authorities. In general, they are conservative groupings and are one of the major reasons why the teacher training departments in five polytechnics have not produced any radical alternatives to the basic three-year concurrent teacher training course. It was hoped that the existence of the Council for National Academic Awards (CNAA) might offer some colleges or polytechnics an alternative structure whereby innovation, especially at B.Ed. level, would occur. If the teaching profession genuinely wants a degree in education which expresses teaching expertise and knowledge, as well as offering teachers better status and career prospects, then it would seem reasonable to assume that the CNAA option would be pursued vigorously. However, the NUT has been extremely cautious in its approach to the CNAA. The Union's teacher education document expressed concern over the standards required by the CNAA:

Undoubtedly, many colleges would like to offer CNAA degrees in education. They are unable to do so, however, because of inadequate departmental specialization, a paucity of library and laboratory provision and deficiency of highly qualified staff. The Union hopes that the Board of Education of CNAA will adopt the flexibility of approach and demonstrate the enlightened thinking that have distinguished the other boards of the Council in the establishment of new degrees without the lowering of academic or professional standards.

It is strange that a teachers' union should ask a degree-awarding body to adjust its requirements, especially regarding highly qualified staff, rather than ask the DES to make sure that future policies encourage the recruitment of such staff to the training colleges. However, the above argument is merely a rationalization of traditional Union policy. This places the continuing role of the universities above any need to encourage alternative means of developing a better degree. The NUT also rejects innovation in initial training based on 'sandwich-course principles'. The teacher education document argues that such an approach is to be resisted because 'the student teacher . . . needs to be in close and continual contact with his tutors in order to be able to assess the professional significance of each educational experience'. This attitude reveals not only an untold ignorance of a properly controlled and structured sandwich course, but also a distrust and dislike of modes of study not traditionally associated with the universities. Sandwich-type courses are also rejected by the NUT because it is thought that 'dilution' will occur in the 'filling period' when the student is in schools. The NUT policy on the Open University is rather different. 'The union is particularly gratified at the development of the powerful and enterprising education studies faculty.' There is no evidence that the Open University will offer a degree to teachers either making their skill and experience more valid or encouraging educational change.

All this cannot be reduced to a matter of being either pro-university or pro-CNAA. Teaching is an increasingly skilled job which requires its own specially designed degree. From this central concern it is then appropriate to question the sufficiency of existing structures under the universities and Area Training Organizations. The profession should reject the quasi-respectability of the present system and concentrate rather on securing even for a few colleges and polytechnic departments the autonomy needed for designing a professional degree. If such a framework rests on the CNAA or some new degree-awarding body, then so be it. The gravest disservice to teachers has already been done by waiting and hoping for the universities to take a proper initiative. The idea that the profession is simply a group of second-class citizens will be ended when initiatives are taken by the teachers themselves, not only on salary matters but more importantly on the issue of a professional degree. The profession has to decide whether it wants limited reform with extension of status for some teachers, or a reappraisal of traditional training and the structure of the profession.

The 'general teacher' concept needs rethinking in view of the increasing complexity of schools. So does the accepted relationship between this concept and status. So do the causes of teacher immobility. The broad policy which demands a vast increase in supply and an improvement in quality of student entry needs to be worked out as a whole, and not as two distinct policies. The profession sees itself correctly as a growth industry. At present it is willing to gamble on the hope that its traditional senior partner in the training process, the university, will voluntarily adapt to this salient social fact, but the closing of options here is professional suicide.

The training of teachers has for too long served the need for an economic, steady and safe supply of teachers. The profession has the organizational strength to challenge this historical debasement of educational values. Present professional policies seek consolidation, with limited extensions of privilege and reform. The profession, and the NUT in particular, needs a policy which not only provides the schools with more confident and skilled teachers, but also more genuinely improved teacher status. The profession's present view of its future and best interests needs to be challenged because it is essentially based on contradictory and unattainable objectives.

Reference

1. NUT, 'Teacher education – the way ahead', discussion document, 1970. This is now superseded by a newer document, but there is little evidence of any basic change of policy.

6 Degrees for Teachers
Eric E. Robinson

The opportunity to read for a degree is greatly coveted by teachers and students in teacher training. There are basically two reasons for this: firstly, the quality of education associated with degree study and, secondly, the status (and associated opportunities and salary) of a graduate. Those who are complacent about our society and its education system do not find it necessary to distinguish between these; in their world the graduate has better opportunities and higher status because he is better educated than the non-graduate. I distinguish them because I believe that the distinction between the graduate and the non-graduate has a social content and is not merely based on educational attainment or potential. Modern sociological research indicates that the so-called distinction of educational level between the academic and the non-academic child is often effectively a distinction between children of different social backgrounds. The distinction between the graduate and the non-graduate teacher corresponds to this. Non-graduate teachers, on the whole, come from lower social class backgrounds than graduate teachers and they generally teach children of lower social classes. A major element in the demand of school teachers and students for degrees is the clamour for social status.

The attainment of a degree has two distinct aspects. Historically the degree signifies status in the university community: members of the university have rights and privileges according to their 'degree'. Many graduates of Oxford and Cambridge, our oldest universities, continue to exercise their membership of their college and of the university throughout their lives. They revisit their college and participate in university elections and other decisions. The more recently established universities continue some of these practices but usually as a mere formality. The graduate traditionally had a special status in the world outside the university. As recently as 1945 university graduates, in recognition of their superior 'degree', had a second, university, vote in parliamentary elections. Former students at colleges outside the universities had no such special status.

The holders of college certificates have never been regarded or treated in this way. Clearly the struggle of teachers for social status through membership of the university community and the allocation of degrees within that community has a sound historical basis. The recent expansion of the universities has not reduced the social significance of a degree. Indeed it has recently been reaffirmed – by the development in the 1960s of the new universities with their emphasis on the university as a community of scholars (which was much weaker in the red-brick universities that grew in the early part of the century), by the exclusion from the universities of students not regarded as suitable for reading for degrees, by the general insistence on membership of the university as a full-time student for three years before a degree is awarded, by the ceremonial and fancy dress that accompanies the degree award.

The award of a degree does also signify some academic achievement. The nature of this achievement in modern times varies very greatly according to the subject or subjects of the degree – a comparatively recent development, it should be noted. There is also considerable variation of practice in the significance attached, on the one hand, to terminal achievement (attainment at the end of the course assessed by examination) and, on the other, to achievement, continuously or discontinuously assessed, during the course. There is an important distinction of principle here. Does the award of a first-class degree in the summer of 1970 signify that the student was a first-class man in the summer of 1970 or that for the three years between 1967 and 1970 he was, over all, a first-class man? The distinction between course and final assessment is not merely one of the methods of examination but of the very meaning of assessment and certification.

Academic achievement may be regarded alternatively as the assimilation of (measured by the ability to reproduce) information and arguments in textbooks and lectures; as the ability to use certain techniques; as the ability to solve problems; as the ability to analyse and comment upon certain problems or situations; or as a combination of these.

Verbalization or mathematical expression is normally essential to academic achievement. The use of techniques or the solution of problems without verbalization are not normally admissible as a demonstration of academic achievement. Let us suppose, to take an extreme example, that a medical student one day produced a cure for cancer in the form of a medical mixture that was found by doctors to be efficacious. This would not in itself be regarded as an academic achievement by that student. For such recognition he would have to give an account of not simply how the medicine was made (in principle that could be easy), but an account of either the analytic process whereby he came to his conclusion or the process by which he verified its validity. The magnitude of the achievement would not be measured by the importance of his discovery but by the weight and sophistication of the analysis that he used in explaining it.

A simpler example is the child who can produce the right answer to arithmetical problems. To obtain the academic credit for this skill he will normally be expected to produce his 'working' and not simply the answer. Exceptional people do exist who can carry out very complicated calculations (such as, for example, multiplying together two ten-figure numbers) in a very short time without any awareness of the method they use. Such a skill does not make them experts in arithmetic in the academic sense. Such eccentric skills are not limited to the mathematical field. Consider the man who has a photographic memory. He may, for example, be able to reproduce on demand the exact text of a book or lecture, but this does not in itself rank as an academic achievement.

This distinction between what is and what is not academic is crucial to our topic and is fundamental to much of the recent discussion of the B.Ed. degree proposed by the Robbins Committee in 1963. The requirements of a professional training (for teaching or any other profession) and those for the award of a degree are, at least to some extent, different in kind. The suggestion (which has sometimes been made) that a degree should be simply substituted for the Certificate awarded at the end of a course of teacher training implies either a modification of our concept of a degree or the substitution of an academic course for the training course. The Teachers' Certificate is (at least it is intended to be) a certificate of competence to teach; a degree is, in principle, not a certificate of competence to *do* anything; at most it is a certificate of competence to write about doing something. In principle, within the conventional concept of a degree, it is possible to get a degree by describing, discussing and analysing teaching and educational problems. In principle it is not possible to obtain a degree by competence in teaching and solving educational problems. To be consistent with the concept of a degree that I have described, such competence cannot even contribute to the qualification for the award of a degree.

This explains why in none of the B.Ed. degree schemes does the competence to teach constitute part of the final assessment. In most universities only students who have obtained a certain level of competence in teaching are permitted to proceed to the final stage of the degree course, but this is rather by way of applying an entrance test to the degree than of including teaching as part of the degree assessment.

This is consistent with the thinking of the Robbins Committee. In its report the first mention of 'education' as a degree subject is in connection with its inclusion in a general degree for university students[1]; the sentence, 'We also think that for some prospective teachers a course involving three main subjects, one of them education, may be appropriate' is footnoted by the sentence, 'By this we mean education studied as an academic subject'. Subsequently in the discussion of the B.Ed. degree[2], it is clear that the Committee regards professional training as quite distinct from the academic study for a degree.

The attitude of the Committee is made most explicit not in the discussion of education but of art[3]:

The question remains whether degrees should be made available for students taking art; *while degrees are not appropriate to mark achievement in executive subjects* [my italics], there are aspects of art, as of music, for which degrees are appropriately given. Any institution that becomes autonomous should itself be able to consider whether to give degrees when the courses are of an appropriate academic nature.

That this is not an outdated or idiosyncratic attitude can be verified by referring to discussions about the B.Ed. degree that have taken place in many university senates in recent years. It was reaffirmed at the Colston Symposium at Bristol in 1968 by Dr (now Sir) Derman Christopherson, the Chairman of the University Vice-Chancellors' Committee:

... it is necessary to start from the question of what the B.Ed. is and what it is for. I think *most university people would agree that the possession of a degree – any degree – is in no sense evidence that a man or woman is a better teacher than a non-graduate*, certainly not so far as the teaching of less gifted children is concerned. The basis of the argument for a different salary is nothing of this kind. The argument, whether one accepts it or not, is that it is in the national interest that a proportion of the most academically able people should enter the schools as teachers. Since in our society academically gifted people in all subjects have a great number of opportunities of making a living in an interesting way, the salaries of graduate teachers must be at least reasonably comparable with what they could get elsewhere. On that basis the argument for the B.Ed. is that there are a number of students in the colleges of education who are academically as able as those in universities and should be given the opportunity to prove it. But *the degree, like any other degree, is a test of intellectual ability of the academic kind. That is all the universities can offer, that is all they know about.* In theory, although we hope it will not happen on a large scale, any holder of a B.Ed. ought to be as qualified to enter any profession – government, administration, business – as the holder of say a degree in history or English [my italics][4].

Thus, to paraphrase Sir Derman, the idea of making it possible for college-of-education students to take a degree is not to make them better teachers, except possibly by improving their knowledge of the academic subjects they teach to more gifted children. Even if education is one of the subjects in the degree curriculum he would not expect this to make the students into better practitioners of education.

This is an extreme view which would not be shared by all university teachers and perhaps Sir Derman himself was, for the purpose of stimulating discussion, deliberately oversimplifying it; but it is a valid statement of the university tradition applied to the problems of this field. And it summarizes very precisely those current university attitudes that limited the concept of the B.Ed. in the *Robbins Report* and the B.Ed. development in British universities during the 1960s. The colleges of education and the teaching profession thus find themselves in a painful predicament. The pursuit of studies designed to promote competence and professionalism in teaching seems to be at the expense of the status and economic benefits of academic pursuits.

The conflict is not, as it might appear, a simple one between moral principle (professional training in the interests of the children in the schools) and self-interest (status for colleges and teachers). If the colleges become predominantly academic institutions rather than professional training colleges, what are their prospects *vis-à-vis* the universities? At best they can hope for incorporation as liberal arts colleges or junior colleges subordinate to the universities. Although this seems to be the objective steadfastly sought by the college teachers through their professional organization (the Association of Teachers in Colleges and Departments of Education), it is by no means certain that this is consistent with the self-interest of many of the college teachers, particularly those in 'non-academic subjects' (such as art) and those in professional subjects, many of whose academic qualifications are negligible.

School teachers also have reasons of self-interest for doubts about this. Collectively they have always sought to raise their status by professionalization, that is, by controlling entry to teaching and restricting it to those who have successfully pursued a course of professional training. To abandon this policy just at the time there are signs of its success would be curious, to say the least. Doctors have retained high status by controlling entry to the medical profession and have found it unnecessary to insist that all doctors are graduates. Many teachers believe that defining professional expertise and excluding those who do not have it would be a more effective way of raising the status of the teaching profession than making the education of all teachers more academic for the sake of the distant prospect of an all-graduate profession. On balance I suspect that given the simple choice between raising real professional standards and raising status by formal academic achievement, the majority of school teachers would opt for the former, not primarily for altruistic reasons nor for reasons of self-interest, but for the not inconsiderable reason of self-respect. The teaching profession is by no means wholehearted in its concern for degrees for teachers so long as the price that has to be paid is at the expense of real professional advance. The key question is: 'Is this choice inevitable?' I believe it is not and I will return to this.

Teachers and prospective teachers can and do read for academic degrees of all kinds. Indeed a substantial proportion of all university graduates enter teaching permanently or temporarily. It is possible to argue that implicit in many academic courses is a training for an academic career and that an academic degree is in itself a form of teacher training. For example, from the viewpoint of those concerned with the use of physics or mathematics in industry, many university degrees in these subjects may seem to be structured much more suitably for intending teachers than for industrial research workers. Those inside the academic community attribute to academic modes of thinking a universality which the outsider does not always recognize. The academic thus regards a training in academic thinking as a training for life, whereas the outsider interprets it as a training only for academic life – the academic way of thinking may be all right for the classroom but it is inadequate for the world outside.

The idea that study for an academic degree in itself constitutes training as a teacher is implicit in the traditional assumption of the elite sector of education (preparatory schools, public schools, universities) that more specific training for their teachers is unnecessary. In this connection a distinction must be made between graduates in school subjects and the growing proportion of graduates whose subjects are not taught in most schools. The range of university study has recently expanded much more rapidly than the range of the school curriculum. Indeed it is possible that in the universities we will see a polarization, particularly in the humanities and the social sciences, between the departments in 'school subjects' such as English literature, history and geography and the departments in other subjects – with the students who are aspirant teachers and academics gravitating to the one side and other students to the other. It could then be that the degree courses in 'school subjects' would become more explicitly oriented to the needs of the teaching profession. Some of the new universities are encouraging this tendency by allowing students to pursue professional studies concurrently with academic studies. There has been some polarization along the lines I mentioned at Keele, where many students have the alternative of training for teaching or the social services concurrently with degree study.

Long before the introduction of the B.Ed. degree a small number of teacher training colleges (e.g. Goldsmiths' College, London) offered some students the opportunity of academic degree study (mainly in school subjects) concurrently with professional study. This was facilitated by a substantial overlap between the academic degree study and the academic (main study) part of the teacher training course.

Many teachers obtained degrees by part-time study whilst in service as teachers. For many others part-time study for a degree has been a route into teaching. Indeed since 1945 the student membership of the degree courses in school subjects at Birkbeck College, London (the one university institution in the country mainly concerned with part-time students), and at numerous technical colleges (preparing students for external London degrees), have consisted mainly of non-graduate practising teachers and people seeking entry into the profession. These courses, and their students, went through a difficult period in the late 1950s and the 1960s for several reasons. During this time there were substantial reforms in university curricula without corresponding reforms in the curricula of schools and colleges of education. In consequence the step from the sixth-form or the training-college course to a university degree became a bigger one – not simply in volume of work but in requiring a qualitative change in approach to study. This was most explicit in the important area of pure science and mathematics. Whereas some of the degree courses of the University of London in 1950 were effectively a continuation of sixth-form studies, they had become by 1960 qualitatively different, thus presenting new difficulties for the part-time student. During the 1960s there was a widespread belief that the days of first degrees by part-time study were numbered. Part-time degree courses were abandoned by the colleges of advanced technology, student numbers declined in other technical college part-time degree courses, and Birkbeck College seriously considered abandoning its preoccupation with part-time students. Only very recently – with the reaffirmation by Birkbeck College of its concern in part-time courses, the establishment of the Open University, and the resurgence of part-time courses in some polytechnics – has the tide turned. Part-time degree courses are on the way back, but necessarily in a different form, because the London external degree system is on the decline, and university degree courses are becoming more idiosyncratic; the Council for National Academic Awards and the Open University are introducing completely new approaches to this problem. Unfortunately, the universities generally remain hostile to the idea of part-time degree courses.

Although teachers and prospective teachers have always been strongly represented among degree students, part-time and full-time, only since the *Robbins Report* have we developed degree courses specially designed for them. These are the B.Ed. degrees, awarded by universities to some students in the colleges of education which belong to that university's Institute of Education. Although the B.Ed.s vary greatly in detail they all conform in conception to the pattern suggested in the *Robbins Report*. This is a general academic degree of (in the final stage) two or three subjects, one of which is education (although in at least one university it has been possible to obtain a B.Ed. degree without studying education at the final stage). The definitive characteristic of a B.Ed. degree is that it is studied in colleges of education concurrently with a teacher training, not that it is a degree in education. The B.Ed. degree course, from a modern academic point of view, generally lacks unity and depth – it has the weakness of the old-fashioned general degree to which I have previously referred, particularly in those universities in which the various subject syllabuses are independently controlled by subject departments, and the student may find little correlation between the several subjects of the course.

The Open University, which has just enrolled its first students, has proved enormously attractive to serving teachers and has demonstrated just how great is the frustration among teachers at the inadequacy of provision for degree study. Unfortunately, although it is too early to make a final judgement, there are signs that the Open University degree will be open to the same objections as the B.Ed., possibly even more so. It seems likely to be conventionally academic in its conception and to be fragmented into subjects having little necessary relationship to each other or to the concerns of its students. Significantly its initial studies are all academic in that they are not based on the student's professional concerns or experience – the route for teachers is undistinguished from the route for other students. Thus, for example, it might be thought that the experience and interests of a teacher would make possible an approach to the study of sociology or psychology quite distinct from the approach used by an engineer or businessman. The academic approach virtually excludes this possibility.

The Open University intends to offer educational studies within its degree programme. The traditionalist academic conception of the university suggests that these educational studies will lean towards 'education as an academic subject' and will be available on the same basis to both teachers and non-teachers. It will be pleasantly surprising if executive achievement as a teacher is assessed as an integral part of the final degree assessment. It is likely that in order to allay fears that the Open University degree will not be of real degree standard – already very difficult as a consequence of its fragmented credit system – it will tend to adopt conventional academic criteria.

The B.Ed. in the colleges of education has a similar problem. Its academic standard has been a cause of great concern in many universities, several of which are willing only to make a pass degree award. In a final degree course that consists of a loose agglomeration of several subjects it is inevitable that the standard in each subject compares unfavourably with that of the single-subject honours degree. The B.Ed. has encountered

difficulties of principle particularly in some of the civic universities in which the single-subject honours degree is most deeply
entrenched.

One of these difficulties concerned the recognition and dis-
tortion of 'non-academic' subjects in B.Ed. courses – subjects
such as handicraft, modern dance, physical education. There
were three difficulties with these: firstly, if these subjects did
not exist in the university there was no yardstick of comparison
for assessing standard; secondly, to make them academic they
had to be talked and written about, not simply carried out;
thirdly, there had to be a separation of the subject itself (which
is conceived as academic) from the teaching of the subject (not
academic) – thus in principle in order to make 'physical education' academic it was necessary to remove the 'education' part of
it. Naturally some of the contortions performed by the universities in dealing with these problems have reduced the whole
process of course planning to a farcical level.

Arguments about the standard of degrees are not easy to
sustain, or to demolish, because there is no one degree 'standard'. Within any one subject, professors may arrive at agreement about standards, although even this is often difficult, but
there is no agreed basis of comparative attainment in different
subjects, particularly subjects that are unrelated such as, for
example, atomic physics and German literature. If there is a
consensus about degree standards in this country it is that of
the attainment of a normal student who has studied full time
for three years after completing the GCE A-level examination
with reasonable success –and this in turn depends upon a general acceptance of parity of standards between different subjects at A-level.

It is because of the difficulty of realistically comparing
standards that academics fall back on formality. Clearly some
students in two years can achieve what it takes others three
years to achieve. But because we have no reliable way of testing achievement, the period of study is needed as evidence of
standard and, therefore, no student is permitted to take a degree
after two years of university study. This in itself could be regarded as a diminution of standards. It is for such reasons that
many universities are concerned, in evaluating the B.Ed., with

the entry qualifications of students in colleges of education. This is the logic that leads some universities to refuse admission to students to B.Ed. courses unless they have university matriculation qualifications – the entry qualification, and not the actual achievement in the course, constitutes the guarantee of standards.

In an educational philosophy that distinguishes rigidly between professional training and academic education, there are clear grounds for objection to the possibility of the student who starts with only O-level qualifications achieving honours degree standard after four years of combined education and training – time must be discounted for his progress from O-level to A-level standard and more time discounted which is spent on training rather than education. The simple solution of this problem if we are concerned only with academic status is to eliminate the 'training' element and convert the colleges of education into liberal arts colleges. The only alternative is to challenge the principle of the separation of training and education by a conception of education that includes the acquisition of executive competence; and to put the assessment of standards on an objective basis in place of the existing method, which is based on time serving by students and horse trading by academics.

It is a startling illustration of the timidity of teachers and professors of education that in the first five years of the development of the B.Ed. degree not one attempt was made to establish a degree course that was a degree in education. At the Colston Symposium the Chairman of the Vice-Chancellors' Committee implied that an academic study of education would not make a man into a better teacher. He is an engineer who would not dream of suggesting that an academic study of engineering would not make a man a better engineer. But not one professor of education has effectively challenged him or the many academics who agree with him. The weakness of the professors of education is that they have not the confidence, backed by substantial achievement in research or educational theory, to establish 'education' as a first-degree study in the way that medicine, engineering and (latterly) business studies are established. But this is the challenge they have to meet, for only in this way will teachers acquire the professional expertise they need for their collective self-respect.

The creation of degrees in education can only seriously begin when colleges and universities frankly accept and embrace the concept of a vocational degree, a degree in which one measure of attainment will be professional competence. The starting point for the design of the curriculum is to analyse the jobs and skills of teachers and other educationalists, as we would like them to be. Only when the objective of the course is defined in these terms does it become possible to plan the course and determine the subjects and topics to be included.

The definition of the teacher's job depends on new empirical work (actually recording what a class teacher does; who has done this?) and new thinking about the school of the future. It involves abandoning the romantic, individualistic idea of the teacher's job in favour of a more realistic one that takes into account the real problems of handicapped and deprived children, difficult mothers, broken homes, bullying headmasters, timid colleagues, inadequate facilities, indifferent governors.

Many students and teachers complain that colleges of education courses include too much theory and not enough down-to-earth practical training. They are wrong and their comment implies an acceptance of an antithesis between thought and action that is inimical to progress and to raising the status of the profession. Such an attitude condemns the teacher to the role of a craftsman – and the craftsman is on his way down and out in this society. There is not too much theory in collges: there is not enough. But the theory offered to students is the wrong theory because it does not assist them adequately in the solution of their problems. Modern teaching of science is conceived as a training in problem solving. A modern course in education should be a course in educational science, training the student to formulate and solve educational problems, inside the classroom and out. Within such a concept there is no conflict between the objective of training a teacher and raising his intellectual level. If the teaching of philosophy, psychology and sociology acquires for the student a value and significance in guiding his actions as a teacher, he has no need of academic main subjects for his personal education. As in other fields of

professional education minutiae of professional practice should
be taught in the field by the senior practitioners. They should
not clutter up the college curriculum. Teachers' training could
learn much from the experience of sandwich-course education
for science, technology and business studies. Here is plenty of
precedent to show the way to a professional education of high
academic standard that is also relevant, practical and down-to-
earth.

Many alternative degree courses for teachers are conceivable
because there are many very different jobs in teaching. The
traditional fear (in the NUT, for example) of different forms
of training for junior and secondary teachers from that of infant
teachers, which now hinders progress because increased
sophistication and specialization of function is necessary, would
be greatly reduced if we designed a degree course especially for
potential infant-school teachers. This could consist of fundamental and related practical studies of young children and the
communities of which they are members; of theories of communication together with substantial specialist studies in such
areas (but not necessarily all) as number, language, music and
art. It could include a substantial element of project work designed and conducted in the field in the form of a teaching
experiment, theoretically based, practically implemented and
evaluated. Such studies, which could undoubtedly be continued
to a very high academic level, would be much more relevant to
the needs of a prospective infant-school teacher than a degree,
for example, in history, geography and education as academic
subjects. It would also constitute a better general education, a
better academic education and a better basis for a career, even
in the world outside education. Similarly, one could conceive
of degree courses in education with specialist studies designed
for teachers in other schools, which would, moreover, be of
value to their graduates if they wished to transfer to other
spheres of employment.

A common complaint among student teachers, particularly
those training to be teachers in primary schools, is that the
course offered to them is highly fragmented and lacking in
intellectual challenge. It typically consists of main academic
studies that seem to bear little or no relationship to the job of a

primary-school teacher, studies in education consisting of academic fragments of history, philosophy and psychology, together with curriculum studies consisting of equally fragmented treatments of methods of teaching numbers, reading, writing, religion and the arts. It is reasonable that the universities are reluctant to award a degree based on such a course. The key to its shortcomings as an academic education is the same as the key to its shortcomings as a professional training – it lacks a sense of priorities, it lacks depth and hence it lacks authority.

If we get the professional education of infant teachers right, if we train our students to be thinking, creative professionals rather than old-fashioned craftswomen, we can then justifiably award a B.Ed. degree for an extended course of professional education. A course which requires prospective infant teachers to devote long hours to studies of classical English literature, the geography of South America, the Napoleonic wars; to the ladylike practice of fine needlework, pottery, weaving and dancing; to playing children's games in the gymnasium and continuing childlike attitudes to the problems of philosophy and religion – may be very nice for those who like that sort of thing, but it is a travesty of higher education and a mockery of professional education. A consequence of teacher training along these lines is that many infant-school teachers have no appreciation of the theoretical basis or the practical problems of the modern techniques of teaching that they are expected to adopt and they have no sophistication of thought about the complex personal and social problems of their children in school and at home. Infant teachers commonly introduce streaming and social discrimination in the classroom without even realizing that they are doing it; many of them are immature children compared with some of the parents they have to deal with; they are confronted with the initial teaching alphabet, cuisenaire rods, family grouping and many other modern ideas sometimes with no knowledge of them at all, and usually with no depth of understanding based on familiarity with the relevant literature. Understanding of such matters as these, based on substantial studies of modern social science and backed by substantial practical work on a coherent theoretical basis, should be the first priority on the training of all infant teachers. A student who was competent on the basis of carefully documented experience in a school to comment intelligently on the relevance of the work of, for example, Douglas, Peters, Bernstein and Daniels to her own classroom problems would be a serious candidate for a degree and a most valuable recruit to many infant schools. Of course infant schools need people who can play the recorder, make papier maché ducks and decorate the classroom, but skills of this kind do not require many years of higher education to be acquired, and they are not the first priority. They are not worthy of the award of a degree, and much work of this kind should be done by technical assistants, not by professional teachers.

Even if the student for infant teaching were to concentrate on fundamentals rather than trivia, the course would be wide ranging, such is the expertise in sociology, psychology, mathematics and linguistics required for competent modern infant-school teaching. For both academic and professional reasons some measure of specialization should be encouraged so that without necessarily abandoning the use of the 'general practitioner' class teacher we can look forward to the time when each infant-school staff includes one teacher who is particularly expert in home–school problems, one in number, one in reading and writing, one in art.

If it is possible to reconcile the professional requirements of infant-school teaching with the intellectual requirements that must be made for the award of a degree, then it can also be done for other teaching in other sectors – nursery, special, junior, secondary and further.

If the concepts of teacher training and degree study were reconciled along these lines it would not be difficult to provide for continuity between studies for a certificate and studies for a degree. This eases the problem of the certificated teacher in service who wants to take a degree, particularly if that teacher has completed a new type of course designed to lead towards a degree. The design of degree courses for teachers in service, however, presents special problems and offers special opportunities. There is no reason simply to offer to teachers in service the same curriculum as that developed primarily for the pre-service student. The in-service student has distinctive needs, interests and experience and the degree course for this should be designed in accordance with them.

The in-service student may attempt a degree by part-time study, by full-time study on secondment, or by a combination of both. Careful consideration should be given to the claims of such students for financial support for periods of full-time study; perhaps young students should not be given the priority over mature students that recently has been customary. Certainly no student is more deserving of a grant than one who has made progress in part-time study at the same time as doing a full-time job of work.

The mature student presents distinctive problems of selection and induction. Formal academic qualifications obtained some years ago are an unreliable guide to the preparedness of a mature person for degree study. Much depends on the prospective student's recent reading, on the intellectual level of his work, and on his spare-time pursuits. In-service courses for teachers must be open-ended at the start, giving each student personal attention until he can become assimilated into a group with whom he can share his problems of study.

For the student who returns to study after several fallow years, a period of planned induction is vital not only to enable him to settle in but to select an appropriate course of study. Such is the upheaval, both for the student and his erstwhile employer, caused by secondment for full-time study that in most cases it is preferable that the induction period should be one of part-time study or 'block release' study. The latter is a term borrowed from the technical colleges and refers to the growing pattern in technical education of the periodic release of people from work for one or two months of intensive study. This is but one of the many practices of modern education and training for industry from which the educational world has much to learn. It is ironic that teachers have had so much success in persuading industry to take in-service training seriously, but much less success in persuading the education service itself to make the same effort for its employees. When Edward Britton proposed in his Colston Symposium paper in 1968[5] that education should have its own training board, he was met by some teachers of education with a mixture of horror and incomprehension. Since then the Local Government Training Board has been established but does not include teachers within its concern. Unless there is a massive effort of in-service training – something much more substantial than short 'refresher' courses – there is a real danger of the teaching profession being left far behind their colleagues in both the public and private sectors of employment – a bizarre reversal of the traditional position. In 1966 and 1967 at Enfield College, we found that the DES was happy for us to run part-time degree courses in anything for anybody if we could demonstrate there was a demand – except in education for which there were special restrictions! These restrictions have not yet been removed and at least one college has been told by the Inspectorate that a part-time B.Ed. course cannot be offered for the teachers in its area because this would be unfair to the teachers in other areas!

School teachers in service need degree courses designed to meet their needs and the needs of the school. The experience and the motivation of the teacher is the raw material on which the academic teacher has to draw and to build in designing the degree curriculum. Whatever the subject of study – psychology, sociology, literature, science, mathematics – the experienced teacher does not start from scratch and he does not start from the same position as the eighteen-year-old student. The teacher who has for a number of years taken a keen interest in his colleagues, his pupils and their parents has his own ideas about psychology, its problems and its methods; these may be home-spun and non-academic, but they are not irrelevant. The teaching of psychology to the teacher must start from these ideas. A course in psychology that starts by returning him to the academicism of his initial training that for sound practical reasons he has rejected is worse than useless, however valid it may be in the conventional academic context.

To offer, as we sometimes do, the same course in child psychology to the mother of three or the teacher of forty children, as we offer to the eighteen year old, preoccupied with his new-found sexuality, is an insult and a folly. As any primary teacher knows, the interest and the awareness of the pupil is the basis of good teaching. Teachers in higher education have to learn this.

The degree course for the experienced teacher must start with his problems and his aspirations; but where does it go from there? It must go on to help him to solve his problems and realize his aspirations; but it must go further in helping him to reformulate his problems, to discover new problems, to revise his aspirations and to raise his sights. It must give him accesss to the riches of our academic inheritance; we must not throw out the baby with the bath water. But more than ever the graduate in any academic discipline needs discrimination. It is no longer enough, indeed it is no longer possible, simply to 'know the subject'. In every academic field we have a hundred books and a thousand papers where twenty or thirty years ago there were only two or three. The key to discrimination is purpose – the purpose of the student – not (as so often passes for discrimination in the modern university department) the personal interest or idiosyncrasy of the professor. This means that the course of study, whilst losing nothing concerned with academic fundamentals and intellectual quality, must be dominated throughout by its concern with the problems of teachers and educationalists.

The experienced teacher can more definitely state his academic and career interests than the eighteen-year-old student. It would be inappropriate to design a course for a young student on the assumption that he will become a headmaster, an LEA education officer, an inspector, a careers master, a subject adviser, an education lecturer or any one of the many more specialist functions that must be developed in a modern educational system. But it is both possible and highly desirable that experienced teachers should in their further studies anticipate such specialist roles. Indeed it is inevitable. University teachers may interpret their courses as teaching the academic disciplines, but their mature students interpret them as a training for their next step up the career ladder.

I am thus suggesting that not only the approach but also the content and the endpoint of degree courses for experienced teachers should be quite different from the degree courses of initial training. Initial-training degree courses should be closely related to the job of class teachers in nursery, primary, secondary and further education respectively. Degree courses for experienced teachers should *and can* be similarly related to the jobs of senior responsibility in the service.

Regrettably, the poverty of the initial training we have given to so many teachers now in service is such that the early stages of in-service degree courses must emphasize the basics of academic study – how to read, how to write, how to argue, no less. But in the later stages they must concentrate on the needs of the job, and there is no need to apologize for this. Education officers need an insight into economics, politics and administration; education lecturers need sophistication in psychology, sociology and philosophy; educational research workers (and we need many of these who are firmly based in a real classroom) need an intensive study of relevant theory and methods; a senior subject teacher in secondary or further education needs a deep insight into the philosophical aspects of his subject and into the place of his subject in contemporary culture, in the widest sense of that term.

A major part of any first-degree course for mature teachers should be project work that gives the maximum possible scope for the student to direct his own work and to base it on developmental problems in the field. It should be not only possible but positively encouraged for a student to include in degree study experimental school-based projects in such things as school administration, curriculum development and school–community relations.

The acceptance and encouragement of practical development projects is even more important in the award of higher degrees (M.Ed., M.Phil., Ph.D.) in education. The academic arts faculty tradition has hitherto dominated many, if not most, university education departments, with a resulting proliferation of higher degree theses that are all too frequently irrelevant to the development of the education service. Many teachers registering for higher degree study find that they are deflected by academics (who sometimes have little experience or interest in the grass-roots problems of education) away from developmental studies in real problems on to academic contemplation – the endless and purposeless study of existing literature. A typical example of this is a junior-school teacher of my acquaintance who has a record of substantial achievement of innovation in the teaching of reading and writing. He was accepted as a M.Ed. student on condition that he abandoned his studies of these problems (about which the university education department knew little and cared less) in favour of a study of children's literature of the past.

One of the most important functions of a first degree is that it prepares its students for higher-degree studies and post-graduate research. All first-degree courses must, therefore, include an emphasis on the methods of study and research, and the project element of the first degree must be conceived as a training in method. One of the strongest objections to most of the existing B.Ed. and other liberal arts degree courses is that they fail to do this. This is evidenced by the reluctance of many universities to regard B.Ed. degrees (especially those of other universities, of course) as adequate qualifications for entry for higher-degree studies in education.

Degree courses for teachers should be characterized by a preoccupation with 'educational science' and this means an abandonment of the idea of educational studies as a smattering of the humanities leavened with an admixture of low-level educational philosophy and outdated psychology. Many members of university senates rightly believe that the introduction of the B.Ed. degree in its present form represents a threat to academic standards. The safeguard against this is to create degrees in education that consist of rigorous studies in the scientific disciplines relevant to the practice and development of education.

The major practical difficulty in the way of this is the shortage of teachers in colleges and departments of education who are able to plan and run such courses. Adequate support for such courses could come only from substantial teams of teachers with expertise in all aspects of educational science; the efforts and initiatives of individuals are not enough. The non-existence of such teams explains the general failure to develop degree courses in education. It should, in principle, be possible to find the teachers to constitute such a team in a university that has strong departments of education and the social sciences, but here we strike the difficulty that in most universities the departmental and faculty barriers seems to prevent such a development. Even in the new universities that have no departments or faculties, the professors of education seem to have had little success in involving professors of other disciplines in the design of essentially new degrees in education.

The other big obstacle to the development of a degree in education is the resistance in the universities to the principle of awarding degrees for executive accomplishment – expressed in the emphatic Robbins statement that education studied within a degree course must be an academic study of education.

The way to overcome that staffing difficulty is, in the first instance, to concentrate development of a few strong points, to create large education departments that will concentrate their efforts on this task, preferably in institutions in which the ready cooperation of social science departments is available. Such education departments must make a strong postgraduate teaching effort, because they will have to train the college and university teachers needed to expand education degrees in other institutions. In an ideal world, in which excellent universities provide educational leadership for other institutions, this is the obvious function of university education departments and, indeed, some of them might eventually grow to fulfil such a function. Unfortunately, many of them will not readily throw off their anti-scientific heritage, and others may fail to overcome the conservative forces within the university. Only the largest and academically strongest colleges of education could attempt development as strong points. Those which have the potential for this, such as Goldsmiths' College, London, and Didsbury College, Manchester, would possibly be the best centres for it. However, at the present time, the growth of these colleges is limited by the Government's lunatic policy of egalitarianism between colleges of education, and their academic effort is to some extent dissipated by the necessity to pursue both professional and liberal-arts goals. Their development as strong points of excellence in educational studies and research would depend on a Governmental decision to give them priority on expansion over other colleges and departments of education, freedom from DES interference in curriculum, and resources for educated research.

All this would be to no avail unless these colleges were also freed from the dead hand of control by the existing university

Institutes of Education. To expand Didsbury to do a job which Manchester University Education Department is clearly incapable of would obviously be nonsensical without liberating it from the conservative control of the Manchester Institute of Education. Some of the enthusiasts of Goldsmiths' are now talking about a University Charter and basing this on an assumption that the way to achieve it is to abandon or reduce their preoccupation with educational studies. A shrewd Government would offer Goldsmiths' a promotion in status, conditional upon the adoption of a policy of concentrating even more on educational studies. The obvious and simple way to bring this about is to designate these colleges as polytechnics and to encourage them to develop their degree courses within the framework, much less restrictive than that of the established universities, of the Council for National Academic Awards.

Under a Royal Charter and under the presidency of the Duke of Edinburgh, the CNAA awards degrees (ordinary, honours and higher degrees) to students pursuing approved courses in colleges outside the universities. The courses are designed by the colleges for approval by the Council. The examinations are run by the colleges with the participation of external examiners appointed by the colleges and approved by the Council. Approximately 20,000 students are now reading for the Council's degrees. Proposals for degrees in education or degrees including the study of education are considered and can be approved by the Council's education committee. This committee consists largely of teachers in colleges and departments of education and is chaired by Sir Derman Christopherson, Vice-Chancellor of the University of Durham. The Council and its committees are predisposed in favour of degree courses that place a strong emphasis on vocation. The committees that approve courses for B.A., M.A., B.Sc., M.Sc., and research proposals for M.Phil. and Ph.D., are extremely busy. The education committee that has power to approve courses for B.Ed. and M.Ed. is virtually unemployed: during the academic year 1969–70 it met only once, in July 1970. Despite the frequently repeated encouragement of Secretaries of State, only three colleges of education have made a firm proposal to the CNAA for the approval of a B.Ed. course. Extraordinary political pressures have been applied to discourage colleges from obtaining CNAA recognition for degree courses in education. But the CNAA remains the main hope for the development of the new degrees in education that are needed.

The most practicable way for these degree courses to be developed quickly and well would be by a joint effort of leading colleges of education and polytechnics – the colleges providing the expertise in education and experience in teacher training, the polytechnics providing academic support and experience of developing vocationally oriented degree courses. Only traditions, pride and prejudice stand in the way of such cooperation. The alternative, and very much a second best, is for polytechnics and colleges of education to each go it alone to the CNAA.

The needs of the students, the teachers and the children are in this case clear enough. We need degree courses designed to encourage and train better teachers. Surely it is not beyond the wit of man to decide that institutional and academic fears and jealousies shall be permitted no longer to stand in the way of this.

References

1. Committee on Higher Education, *Higher Education* (*Robbins Report*), HMSO, 1963, p. 92.

2. Committee on Higher Education, *Higher Education* (*Robbins Report*), HMSO, 1963, para. 333, p. 114.

3. Committee for Higher Education, *Higher Education* (*Robbins Report*), HMSO, 1963, p. 144.

4. 'Towards a policy for the education of teachers', Colston Papers, no. 20, Butterworth, 1969, pp. 158–9.

5. 'Towards a policy for the education of teachers', Colston Papers, no. 20, Butterworth, 1969, p. 189.

7 Teacher Training within Higher Education*
Tyrrell Burgess

The administration of teacher education has its roots in history. Of course, at a time when education was carried on privately in almost family-sized groups, in the Dame schools with which the history of modern education always starts, there were no formal arrangements for training teachers at all. But this cosy situation could not continue after the 1830s, when the State began to assist the voluntary efforts of the Churches in educating people on a large scale. The problem was how to find enough teachers in a largely uneducated population. It was solved, abroad and in England, by the method known as the 'monitorial system', advocated here by Joseph Lancaster – who called it 'a new mechanical system for the use of schools' – and Andrew Bell. The system was simplicity itself: the older children in a school taught the younger. As Andrew Bell said, 'give me twenty-four pupils today and I will give you twenty-four teachers tomorrow'. The system was cheap, and it meant that the absence of teachers did not entirely mean an absence of education. It lasted for a generation because there was nothing better to be done, and attempts to establish a training college for teachers broke down because of the opposition of religious denominations. By the middle of the century, improvement became possible. The depressing state of education brought to light by the inspectors of schools led to a public outcry and the establishment in 1846 of a scheme of apprenticeship for pupil-teachers. The essence of this was that the pupil-teachers were apprenticed for five years to schools recommended by the inspectors. Both the masters taking the apprentices and the apprentices themselves were given grants. Training colleges were at last to be established to which the apprentices should go,

* The research on which the early part of this chapter is based was carried out in the Higher Education Research Unit at the LSE, under a grant from the Ford Foundation.

with financial assistance; and there was a syllabus of training for them with annual examinations. The regulations laid down standards which must be achieved by both the schoolmaster and the schools if they were to take on an apprentice.

It seems to us today to have been a fairly meagre advance – but it had one important consequence. In setting up special training colleges for those who were to educate the children of the poor, the Government in the middle of the nineteenth century started a division in education which has lasted until today. The universities have not seen themselves as being concerned with the general education of teachers for the younger age groups, except in schools for the middle and upper classes. Most teachers, teaching most children, have not had a university education.

After a twenty-five-year attempt to improve the quality of school teaching by a method of 'payment by results' (in introducing the scheme in the House of Commons in 1863, Robert Lowe said 'I cannot promise the House that this system will be an economical one and I cannot promise that it will be an efficient one, but I can promise that it shall be one or the other. If it is not cheap it shall be efficient; if it is not efficient it shall be cheap'), the Cross Commission, reporting in 1888, tried again with teacher training. Unhappily the Commission was split. A minority of eight members deplored the pupil-teacher system, calling it 'the weakest part of our educational machinery'. They agreed with one of the witnesses who said: 'It is at once the cheapest and the very worst possible system of supply' and 'It should be abolished root and branch'. The majority, on the other hand, were convinced by those who said that the pupil-teachers were 'on the whole the best as well as the main source of the supply of certificated teachers'. It was said that students in the training colleges who had been pupil-teachers had the greater practical experience.

Again, the minority wanted to lengthen the training-college course from two to three years (an objective achieved a mere seventy years later), to give training-college students some time in universities and to extend teacher training in non-residential colleges. The majority supported these ideas in principle or as experiments, but doubted if a third year was advisable, believed that the experience of university would merely cause disgruntlement, and insisted that residential training was best. And behind all this the denominational struggles echoed on, bedevilling attempts to get more Government grants for teacher training.

A consequence was that when Mr Balfour introduced his Education Act of 1902 he was forced to say:

Any child who wishes to become a teacher gets made a pupil-teacher, and when he has reached that status half his time goes to teaching and the other half ... to learning. ... What is the result? ... I find that 36 per cent have never got through the examination for the certificate, and that 55 per cent of the existing teachers have never been to a training college of any sort.

So it was one of the objects of the 1902 Act to provide an extensive system of teacher training.

What the 1902 Act did was to establish that the preliminary education and training of teachers was a form of secondary, not elementary, education. The new local education authorities could make their secondary schools available for the education of pupil-teachers, and more and more independent pupil-teacher centres became attached to secondary schools. The minimum age for the recognition of a pupil-teacher in urban areas became sixteen, and all pupil-teachers had to be relieved from teaching for at least half their time. However, in 1907 the Board of Education's general report on the instruction and training of pupil-teachers said this system disorganized the education of the pupil-teachers and doubted whether the experience of class teaching and management which the pupil-teacher gained outweighed the disadvantages. An alternative scheme provided that pupils of sixteen and over who wished to become teachers were eligible for grants to enable them to stay at school until seventeen or eighteen when they could enter a training college or become student teachers for a year before entering college. Between the ages of twelve and sixteen a pupil might receive a scholarship from his local authority, which was usually given on condition that he undertook to become a teacher. This kind of 'pledge' became a feature of a good deal of financial support for student teachers, although the age at which the commitment had to be made was gradually raised from twelve to eighteen or later.

Another consequence of the 1902 Act depended on the power it gave to local education authorities to spend money on the training of teachers. In 1904 a new type of college, the municipal training college, was recognized. From the outset the local education authorities were able to offer better salaries and conditions of employment in their own colleges than were available in the voluntary ones. After a confused start, two familiar and tenacious patterns of training teachers emerged in the first quarter of the century: a two-year course of training at a college for teachers in elementary schools, and a one-year course following graduation for teachers in secondary schools. In the colleges the syllabuses were prescribed by the Board of Education and the final examination of the students was conducted by His Majesty's Inspectors. This system was modified after the *Burnham Report* of 1925, and the conduct of the final examination of students was transferred to joint boards set up by the colleges and the universities. This promising idea was briefly revived, as we shall see, by the minority on the McNair Committee whose deliberations accompanied the great debates leading to the 1944 Education Act.

The *McNair Report* was in many ways a substantial advance. It recommended higher salaries for teachers and said that the course of training should last three years. It recommended an end to the system whereby grants to attend a training college were available only to those who signed the 'pledge' that they would teach. It also condemned the ban on married women teachers. It was agreed that the hundred individual colleges should be grouped in areas 'to produce a coherent training service'.

But it is since the *McNair Report* that there has been the present division between the arrangements for the administrative and financial control of the colleges and those for the oversight of their academic development. The former is in the hands of the Department of Education and Science, the local education authorities and the governing bodies; the latter the responsibility of the Institute of Education and the colleges. Of course, there is a good deal of overlap. An expansion of the system, determined by the Department, has implications for the Institutes; and the character of courses may have a significance for teacher supply. The need for consultation is written into the Training of Teachers Regulations, 1967. The local authorities and the voluntary bodies are represented on the governing bodies of Institutes, and the Institutes are represented on college governing bodies and so on.

It is convenient to start with the academic work of the colleges. This is supervised and coordinated by Institutes (sometimes termed Schools) of Education acting as Area Training Organizations. The purpose of the ATOs is defined in the regulations as that of 'supervising the academic work of member institutions, securing cooperation among training establishments in its area, advising the Secretary of State on the approval of persons as teachers in schools, and promoting the study of education'. The Institutes are responsible for the content and standards of a college course, for approving syllabuses and for conducting examinations. They are a medium for planning the total training provision of an area and the means through which college courses are adjusted to the needs of teacher supply. They coordinate arrangements for teaching practice and they regulate the exceptional admission of students with less than or more than the required academic qualifications. They also provide libraries and in-service and other short courses.

In effect the Institutes have followed half the McNair Committee in creating an organization which brought the training colleges into a close and subordinate relationship with the universities. The McNair supporters of university Schools of Education said that they

... did not believe that any area system for the training of teachers can be effective unless those who shoulder the responsibility derive their authority from a source which, because of its recognized standards and its standing in the educational world, commands the respect of all the partners concerned, and which, because of its established independence, is powerful enough to resist the encroachment of centralization. The universities embody these standards and have this standing and this independence.

They added that 'quite apart from these considerations the universities have an obligation to the whole educational system'.

This solution was not inevitable. The other half of the Mc-Nair Committee thought there should be a development of the joint-boards scheme. In this, the university department and the training colleges would have preserved their identity and would have joined in assessing each other's students. Its supporters said that 'the joint-boards scheme is more flexible than the university School of Education scheme; it involves an association of equals in the discharge of a common task instead of making the training colleges depend on the universities'. The rejection of this obvious truth has been a tragedy for teacher education.

Each Institute of Education has its governing body, whose members include representatives nominated by the senate together with those of member colleges and of the local authorities in the area. In many cases vice-chancellors preside. The governing bodies are responsible for the whole work of the Institutes, and since their ultimate authority is derived from the senate, the universities concerned assume the responsibility for the standards of work in the colleges. Below the Institutes' governing bodies there are academic or professional boards composed in the main of members of the training colleges, of the university department of education, and other university members. These are concerned with academic matters, especially syllabuses. Some members are appointed ex officio, others elected by the teaching staff of the colleges and the department of education. The director of the Institute presides. Assessors from the Department of Education and Science are present at meetings both of the governing bodies and of the academic boards of the Institutes.

Detailed work on syllabuses is carried out through a system of boards of studies composed of the college lecturers on the subject together with their opposite numbers from the university department of education, and some representatives from the relevant subject department of the university. These sometimes lay down uniform syllabuses, but they more usually consider syllabuses put up by individual colleges. The boards of studies also nominate internal and external examiners. Within the colleges themselves it is becoming normal for there to be academic boards and boards of studies in individual subjects to manage the colleges' academic work. Although these boards may comment upon administration and finance, power in these matters resides with the principal and governing body.

As far as administration and finance is concerned, training colleges are administered either by local authority or by voluntary bodies. The authorities own and maintain their colleges in the same way as their schools and other institutions. Since the Education (No. 2) Act, 1968, however, they have relinquished numerical control of governing bodies and appointment of their clerks and have given the governors power to spend under broad headings of estimates.

The voluntary colleges are direct-grant institutions getting almost 100 per cent of their recurrent expenditure from the Department of Education and Science. Their annual estimates are subject to approval by the Department, and the colleges are then free to spend within five broad heads. The Department pays 80 per cent of capital expenditure on expansion. Each college has its own governing body which is independent except so far as a parent body may control capital finance or staff be subject to the discipline of a religious order.

But behind the local authorities and the voluntary bodies is the Secretary of State and the Department of Education and Science. In contrast to its provisions on further education, the 1944 Education Act lays upon the Secretary of State for Education and Science specific duties for the training of teachers. Section 62 says that he shall

... make such arrangements as he considers expedient for securing that there shall be available sufficient facilities for the training of teachers for service in schools, colleges and other establishments maintained by local education authorities, and for that purpose [he] may give to any local education authority such directions as he thinks necessary requiring them to establish, maintain or assist any training college or other institution or to provide or assist the provision of any other facilities specified in the direction.

In other words, in further education, as with schools, the initiative rests with the local education authority. So far as colleges of education are concerned, the initiative rests with the Secretary of State. Of course a number of colleges of education are owned by voluntary bodies and are aided by the local authorities. The rest have been established and maintained by the local authorities. Funnily enough, the Secretary of State has never given any specific directions about the establishment of these colleges and so the precise legal basis of the local-authority colleges is somewhat vague.

The Education (No. 2) Act, 1968, laid down that in colleges of education there should be an instrument providing for the constitution of a body of governors. Such an instrument was to be made by order of the local authority with the approval of the Secretary of State. The articles of government, determining the functions to be exercised by the local authority, the body of governors, the principal and the academic board if any, were also to have the approval of the Secretary of State.

There is another kind of legal requirement which affects colleges of education. This appears in the Rate Support Grant (Pooling Arrangements) Regulations, 1967. These regulations provide for the pooling of expenditure of all local education authorities on teacher training (as well as on advanced further education and the education of pupils who do not belong to the area of any authority) and for the adjustment of the rate-support grants in order to distribute the expenditure amongst all local education authorities. The aggregate amount of the actual expenditure in providing teacher training is apportioned among all local education authorities in proportion to their school population.

The Secretary of State also issues regulations governing colleges for the training of teachers: the Training of Teachers Regulations, 1967, as subsequently amended from time to time. These lay down that the initial training for a qualified teacher shall be not less than three years in a college of education, not less than one year of postgraduate training. They also provide for the supervision of the academic work of colleges by Area Training Organizations approved by the Secretary of State, and provide for representation of the universities, colleges of education and LEAs within the area. The regulations also give the Secretary of State quite detailed powers. He may give directions, after consultation, as to 'the numbers and categories of students to be admitted' to any particular college. Equally, it is the LEA that has to be satisfied about the suitability of a particular applicant for a course in a college of education. The regulations also lay down both a minimum age and the minimum qualifications of students entering the colleges.

In other words, the colleges of education are subject to very many more detailed regulations involving more detailed ministerial control than are schools or colleges of further education. What is more, the Secretary of State's functions give him not only these additional powers but also the power to initiate in teacher training.

The educational consequences

These administrative arrangements have important educational consequences. First, the education of teachers takes place in 'mono-technic' institutions which are effectively isolated from the rest of higher education. Second, their vulnerability to Government demand has meant that over the years their chief preoccupation has been with accommodating ever larger numbers of students. Third, in so far as they have links, through the universities, with higher education they are subject to pressures which are irrelevant to their major purposes. These three sets of consequences are all linked, but it is convenient to take them in turn.

The isolation of the colleges is, as we have seen, explicable in historical terms though it is almost impossible to defend academically. For example, the very names 'university' and 'polytechnic' imply an educational view that it is best for students in higher education to be educated alongside others in different disciplines. Indeed it would be argued that contact between students taking different subjects is an essential part of higher education. All kinds of devices, some of them very expensive, have been evolved to encourage this, from colleges at Oxford and Cambridge to student unions and extra-curricular activities elsewhere. Until fairly recently, a concentration on even a fairly wide group of disciplines, like applied science and technology, was held to disqualify technical colleges from aspiring to full university status. When the University Grants Committee decided to inhibit the development of the social sciences in universities which had been colleges of advanced technology the victims' astonishment derived partly from the realization that they had more academic freedom when directly controlled by a Government department than they had through the UGC, but partly from what must have seemed a cavalier denial of a hundred-year-old assumption about what constituted a university.

In teacher education the isolation is especially serious, for two reasons. The first is that potential teachers may never escape from 'education'. They go from school to college and from college back to school without any contact with life outside. One need not overestimate the extent to which students in different disciplines mix and influence each other in other universities and colleges, but the possibility of doing so is there. It does not exist in a college of education.

The second defect of isolation is that it limits the intellectual contacts of the staffs of colleges of education. They come to depend academically upon the one university Institute of Education. In other words, they not only miss regular contact with university teachers in other disciplines; their relationship with university teachers, even of education, is actually impeded. In these circumstances very few of the colleges escape academic parochialism.

The second educational implication of the administrative structure is that for a decade or more the colleges have been vulnerable to Government pressure to accommodate ever increasing numbers of students. Their achievement here is astonishing. The numbers in colleges have more than doubled in the past five years alone. Much of this expansion has taken place without extra building resources. It may be argued that such responsiveness was right, in the interests of the schools, but to be quite happy about it one would need to assume that the decisions of the Department of Education and Science were rational and thoughtful and related to the interests of the students. Indeed, the staff of colleges and especially the principals had grave doubts about expansion until the salaries of both principals and vice-principals were related to a capitation grant based upon student numbers. It is becoming clear, however, that the quality of discussion within the Department has been rather low, based upon crude and misleading statistical projections about the demand for teachers. And since the death of the National Advisory Council on the Training and Supply of Teachers there has not even been that innocuous public check upon Governmental assumptions affecting the life of the colleges. Certainly the Department seems to have shown only an incidental interest in the quality of teachers being produced by the colleges, whether this is measured in terms of the qualifications of entrants or of the level of work expected of them. Even the famous decision to lengthen the training-college course from two years to three was taken for reasons of supply and demand, to be rationalized later as an opportunity to increase quality. The more recent decisions to require specified subjects at O-level and to require that graduate teachers be trained can also be seen as a tentative response to a fear that we shall have 'too many' teachers.

But the preoccupation with colleges cannot, of course, be confined to administrators. The colleges themselves have been subjected to great strain. The last ten years have not been propitious for thinking deeply about the fundamental purposes of teacher education. It has been as much as most colleges can do to accommodate the extra students and educate them to something like the standards they remembered from the past. There may be other reasons for the lack of profound educational thinking in the colleges. But one of the most important has been the sheer pressure of work.

The third consequence of the administrative situation of the colleges is that their academic aspirations are determined by the universities. This is perhaps the most serious consequence of all. I have written elsewhere[1] about the existence of two traditions in British higher education. The first, which I call the 'university tradition', is academic and exclusive. It is concerned, to put it crudely, with the preservation, extension and dissemination of knowledge 'for its own sake'. It is on the whole educationally conservative. It gives at least as high a value to research as to teaching. The other tradition I call the 'technical-college tradition'. This is inclusive or 'comprehensive'. It is concerned not with knowledge for its own sake but with vocational and professional education – even with 'mere' vocational training. It is educationally innovative: the only major innovation in higher education this century has been the sandwich course, an invention of the technical colleges. The technical-college tradition is a teaching tradition: research tends to be 'applied' or even a 'service', perhaps to local industry.

It ought to have been a matter of continuous debate which of these traditions was more appropriate for colleges concerned with the training of teachers. In fact, it seems to have been assumed without question, not least by the established senior staff in the colleges themselves, that academic and other links with universities were the only obvious and desirable ones, and this despite the fact that the universities have shown themselves almost wholly inimical to the development of teacher education as a university discipline. Even university departments of education have never been accepted on terms of equality with other departments, still less the colleges, which have been kept not only in tutelage but at arm's length.

Many of the complaints which the schools make about the products of the colleges, much of the disgust which students express about their training, much of the timidity, aridity and conservatism of the colleges can be directly attributed to the influence of the academic tradition. The pursuit of knowledge for its own sake is not a good basis for professional education: at this level it is a recipe for triviality and irrelevance. Perhaps the best example of this can be seen in the development of the B.Ed. degree (which is analysed by Eric Robinson in chapter 6). It is clear that the universities see the B.Ed. not as a way of producing better teachers so much as a way of keeping college students out of the universities, or at best of attracting better people into the colleges of education – where, given many B.Ed. courses, they are promptly turned into worse teachers. In other words, for most colleges, and for most teachers in training, the university connection has been a mistake and often a disaster. The preparation of teachers can best be thought of in terms of the technical-college tradition, and if such thinking became common it would lead to a fundamental reappraisal of the training of teachers in educational terms. It is important to realize the influence which administrative arrangements have had in preventing this fundamental thinking from taking place.

As well as all these educational consequences there is one

political consequence of the administrative structure surround
ing colleges of education. It derives from the direct initiative
which the Secretary of State enjoys – and which she does not
have either in the schools or in further education. Policy is
evolved and implemented almost in private. Because of the
extent of her controls, the Secretary of State can make decisions
and get them implemented as if they were purely administrative
acts. Important educational questions like the length of course,
the balance of training, the qualifications of entrants are
answered almost out of the blue, and the reason is that the
Secretary of State possesses such a battery of controls and such
a direct method of communicating her decisions. No doubt
letters to colleges are discussed in draft with the local authorities and teachers' associations, but the extent of the discussion
is extremely limited.

The situation in the schools and further education is quite
different. Because the Secretary of State's power of initiative is
much less, the evolution of policy goes on much more in public.
A decision to designate polytechnics requires a White Paper,
followed by notes for guidance. A decision about class sizes in
schools elicits an explanatory circular. The difference is an important one of administrative style, and it has helped to explain
why public disquiet about teacher education has not been
matched by public debate. The refusal of successive Secretaries
of State (including the present one) to have a full-scale inquiry
into teacher education which would include questioning of their
own policies and practices is both a symptom of what is wrong
and an unnecessarily brutal emphasis of their determination to
preserve the *status quo*. The situation of teacher education is
such that an informed public discussion of its problems would
entail a revolution in its administrative structures.

An attempt at innovation

Dissatisfaction with teacher education has rarely fastened upon
its administrative roots. Indeed one detects a sense of frustration among forward-looking spirits in the colleges of education
at the apparent resistance of their institutions to change of any
kind. But as so often with plans for reform it is not enough to
show clearly why present practice is wrong and not enough to

call for a change of values and practices among those deeply concerned. People think and act in the way they do partly because of the context in which they find themselves. Thus, to get genuine reform one has to change the context. One has to use administrative and institutional devices to change what people think and do. Fortunately for this chapter there has recently been in teacher training an example of this kind of thing. Since 1965 there have been a number of students in five technical colleges on courses of training as teachers. That this should be happening at all is remarkable, even though it is by no means as remarkable as it could have been. On the one hand, the experiment suggests a new approach to the structure of teacher education and, on the other hand, it demonstrates the pitfalls. We know both what to do and what to avoid.

What could have been a revolution in teacher training has turned out to be a mild and almost pointless innovation. The story is complex but it illustrates a truth, so well understood by Lewis Carroll, that the way a decision is taken affects what is decided. The Department of Education and Science, having screwed itself up to a course of action, then acted in ways which assured its reverse.

The germ of the idea for doing teacher training within the further-education sector came in a note of dissent in the *Ninth Report of the National Advisory Council on the Training and Supply of Teachers*.[2] It was written by Eric Robinson and signed by Vice-Chancellor Carter and Professor John Vaizey. One paragraph reads:

In its Eighth Report the Council recommended that there should be planned recruitment and training of teachers through the further-education sector of higher education – the technical colleges, the colleges of commerce, the colleges of art. Although this sector is rapidly expanding and in fact already recruits students who are seeking a teaching career, the Council's Report make little reference to this contribution to teacher supply. Indeed Chart B implies that this source of teachers is negligible and will remain so. The technical colleges could quickly make a much larger contribution than at present in a number of ways which I have outlined to the Council. The Council has taken the view that this is a field for tentative experiment, no more. In the emergency which now confronts us this is unnecessarily timid.

In Eric Robinson's view there were many advantages of using further education for teacher training. Already students in technical colleges included some who wished to become school teachers. They took external London degrees or the Diploma in Technology, and they might then proceed to a course in a university department of education. Many other technical-college students with the ability to become teachers did not do so because they were given no encouragement nor opportunity. Technical colleges tried to find a vocational interest for students coming in with A-levels or ONC in industry, business, social work and almost anything except teaching.

Even those students who from the start wished to be teachers did not apply for training-college places, because a technical-college course enabled them to concentrate on the subjects which interested them and was staffed and equipped to do so; a technical college offered a better chance of getting a degree; and training-college courses normally offered no qualification which was accepted outside teaching. It was one thing to choose to enter teaching, but quite another to commit oneself irrevocably to teaching at the age of eighteen.

Many of the technical colleges made less than full use of laboratories and specialist staff, partly because they were providing comprehensive facilities within reasonable reach of part-time students. The use of these facilities for teacher training could significantly affect the supply of teachers in critical subjects. Many of the technical-college students had the kind of education and background which the Newsom Committee wanted some secondary teachers to have, but their higher education was little rewarded in a teaching career.

There was a growing interest in educational studies in the technical colleges themselves. Traditionally the colleges offered any course for which there was a demand, and there was growing demand for courses from serving teachers. A number of colleges were particularly interested in modern techniques like programmed learning, computing and language laboratories. Some of them were prepared to train the industrial training officers required under the Industrial Training Act. The development of liberal studies and studies in industrial administration had involved social scientists in the colleges in educational pioneering and there had been some development of educational research.

All this suggested to Eric Robinson a role for technical colleges in the training of teachers, which arose partly from the demand for teachers and partly from the distinctive outlook and traditions of the colleges themselves.

The Department of Education and Science were inclined to agree that the recommendations of the National Advisory Council and of the Robbins Committee implied a continuing shortage of teachers. But when they came to examine Eric Robinson's idea, they were somewhat daunted. The HMIs asserted that the demands of the Industrial Training Act, 1964, and the expansion of advanced work in technical colleges meant that there was very little spare capacity to take on extra commitments. If teachers were to be trained in technical colleges, it would have to be in the long term and not as a way of meeting an immediate emergency.

On the other hand, when they came to think about it, the Department saw the possibility as a way of fulfilling a number of policy objectives. One of these was that Robbins had found single-purpose institutions rather odd. If teachers were to be trained alongside other professions, the technical colleges were an obvious place to do it. One could not, after all, diversify 160 teacher-training colleges overnight. Furthermore, if the polytechnics, foreshadowed in the White Paper of 1966, were to be major institutions of higher education, it would help to introduce the new dimension of teacher training to, at any rate, some of them.

But the Department's thought on this did not go very far or deep. It assumed, for example, that the technical colleges would recruit staff for the new venture from colleges of education. This meant that the new idea should be accommodated within the existing programme for training teachers. It also meant that the Department would not expect the technical colleges to try any new approaches, at any rate at the beginning: thoughts about what the technical colleges might offer were not developed in any great detail. It assumed that eventually the technical colleges would contribute to the theory and practice of teacher training and that teachers trained in technical colleges would probably be less narrow and inbred than others. But there was little hope that the technical colleges might bring some special expertise to part-time training or that there might be a novel development of the sandwich principle. A distinctive contribution was expected only over time.

There was one way in which academic novelty might have been attempted. The academic oversight of the training colleges is undertaken by the university Institutes of Education. Should this oversight be extended to teacher training in technical colleges – or was there another institution which might take it on? At first sight the Council for National Academic Awards was a rational body to do so. Indeed, the Department assumed that colleges would want to evolve courses for the training of teachers leading to a CNAA degree. Unless there were to be some educational innovation in the technical colleges, it was hard to see what purpose was to be served in involving them in teacher training. There was even, for a time, the idea that willingness to undertake CNAA courses should be a condition of approving teacher-training courses in technical colleges. In the end, this was thought to be too much of an interference in the academic freedom of the colleges – but the Department made no attempt to influence where it decided not to dictate. In drawing up the criteria on which colleges would be chosen for the invitation to consider teacher training, the Department ignored all the factors favourable to its own policy.

As the Department envisaged them, the teacher-training units should be substantial enough in size to make them going concerns and offer enough options for students. This meant, say, eight such groups with twelve students in each, or one hundred a year intake and a department of three hundred students. If this were to be accommodated within the teacher-training programme it would have to be confined to half a dozen colleges. The criteria on which these colleges were chosen were largely geographical. They were to be spread over the country as a whole, not concentrated, say, in the south-east. They were to be in places where it was useful to have a teacher-training unit to accommodate surplus day students. (The Department had already decided on another day-training unit in Metropolitan Essex and sought to kill two birds with one stone.) They were to be in large centres of population and should be regional or large area colleges, likely to be designated in the polytechnics in the forthcoming White Paper.

These criteria were almost wholly irrelevant to an educational experiment. The Department should have considered whether the education authorities to be concerned were progressive and ready to experiment. This was not taken into account. One of the authorities, Barking, was a new authority with no experience of teacher training. The Department, one would have thought, would have also been interested in discovering which technical colleges had shown an eagerness to experiment in teacher training. In the event, it decided that it was too difficult to take this into account because it depended on personalities and personalities might change. It feared that an unbalanced system might emerge because colleges which were progressive in one sphere tended to be progressive in all, and there was a danger that the good places would become enormous. Of the colleges chosen, the North-Western Polytechnic had already shown some interest in teacher training and had approached the Inner London Education Authority about it. At Nottingham the Department had suggested the possibility of a day-training college and the city, as a counterproposal, had offered the technical college.

Another obvious criterion, if the Department expected to involve the CNAA, should have been the standing of the colleges with the Council. The astonishing fact is that the Department did not discuss with the CNAA the individual colleges which it had in mind. Only one of them, Sunderland, could be said to be in good standing with the CNAA, with the possibility that Nottingham might have been. The other three colleges had, at the time, no CNAA courses. Indeed, the Department's discussions with the CNAA were not at all productive. The Council had, at that time, no education committee and no board ready to investigate and approve courses. Its officials were anxious not to interfere in the links between institutions training teachers and universities. They assumed that the technical colleges in the new venture would have to work through the Area Training Organizations and the university

Institutes of Education, especially when it came to practical arrangements for lectures, the use of libraries and facilities for teaching practice. At the time, the Council was already very extended in setting itself up and expanding into business studies. It was not anxious to take on the additional complication of teacher training. The Council was not set up to deal with a new kind of course which straddled existing disciplines. At all events, when the five colleges were actually nominated the CNAA lost interest.

What is odd about this is that at no time did the Department see that if it wanted the colleges to choose the CNAA, the least it could do was to give that body time to set up machinery to deal with them. In the event the Department gradually convinced itself that it would be better to avoid a division in the teaching profession created by a different training in technical colleges.

The result of all this was what might have been expected. The teacher-training units set up in the five technical colleges became miniature colleges of education rather eccentrically housed. They were staffed almost wholly by traditional teacher trainers. They all unsurprisingly decided to accept the academic oversight of the local Area Training Organization. Their courses are indistinguishable from those in colleges of education. As one head of an Institute of Education engagingly put it: 'They are all sewn up through the Institutes.'

If such an experiment is to be tried again, or if it should be decided to embark on the administrative reforms proposed later in this chapter, the Department must at least see that the chosen colleges are appropriate, that the CNAA is ready, and that all available instruments of policy are used in its support. If it is right, as Karl Popper says, that institutions are like fortresses – they have to be properly built and *manned* – the least the Department can do is to see that they are properly built.

A new administrative structure

It is now time to suggest what administrative structure is most appropriate for the colleges of education. Most people would regard this as a somewhat remote issue, but it has been the

purpose of this chapter to show that administrative arrangements have educational consequences, that the way in which a
particular sector of education or kind of college is organized
has a profound effect upon what it is able to do. The chapter
has gone further: it has suggested that the arrangements made
after 1944, which have been broadly in line with what people
in the colleges want (even if they did not go far enough), have
acted against the best interests of teacher training and of the
colleges themselves. They have made the colleges the sector of
higher education most vulnerable to shifts in Government
policy. They have inhibited informed public debate about
teacher education. They have increased the isolation of the
colleges and fastened upon the training of teachers a wholly
inappropriate 'academic' bias. What is clearly needed is an
alternative administrative structure.

But here one must put in a caveat straight away. A structure
of administration may be a powerful influence for good or ill
but it is rarely entirely conclusive. In other words, a particular
organization may make a particular development more or less
likely; it cannot always ensure it. One has to allow all the time
for the unintended consequences of one's actions. So in teacher
training, as in politics, the problem is not how to get an ideal
form of government or administration. No such thing exists.
What one has to look for is the form of government most likely
to meet one's requirements. And perhaps more important than
this, one has to acknowledge another problem of administration,
which is how to prevent people administering badly. All this
means that there will rarely be neat and tidy solutions to
administrative problems: indeed the best organizations are
often profoundly untidy. Public policy, for education or anything else, has complex goals, and these can often best be
attained through systems of checks and balances and through
a multiplicity of institutions. With the training of teachers, the
goals are especially complex and the outside bodies with a
legitimate interest in the work of the colleges are many and
various.

For example, the Department of Education and Science must
have a greater interest in teacher education than in other forms
of higher education, because of its responsibilities for staffing

the schools. It is the sole agency with a total oversight of the colleges and must, therefore, be the coordinator of policies with a view to efficiency. The local authorities, too, which administer many of the colleges, are the sole employers of their products. Both the universities and the technical colleges have an interest in the early education of their students, and they are thus really interested in the preparation of school teachers. The students in the colleges are concerned to get for themselves something that can be called a higher education alongside their professional preparation. The teachers' unions recognize that their own work in the interests of their members depends in part upon the way in which teachers are trained. For the staffs of the colleges the need is to balance the demands which all academic institutions make for reasonable independence with the need of society at large to express its own legitimate interests. These conflicting interests are not unique to teacher education, but they are perhaps especially pressing. Can they be accommodated?

In the first place, then, we need to accept the interest of the Secretary of State for Education and Science in the appropriate training of sufficient numbers of teachers for the schools. It would be right, therefore, to leave with her the legal power to direct a local authority to create institutions in which teachers can be trained. In saying this, one has already accepted the view that colleges of education should not be administered directly by the Department of Education and Science. The reason for doing so is not that administration by the Department has occasionally appeared to be tyrannical (for example, in the case of the colleges of advanced technology). On the contrary, it is, first, that the Department is not well set up to administer large numbers of institutions; second, that the local authorities do have a legitimate interest in the training of teachers and are used to administering colleges; and, third (and more arguably), it seems right to continue the principle of dividing responsibility for educational institutions among different levels of State administration.

But in giving the Secretary of State power to direct a local authority to create a college in which teachers might be educated, we must be careful to circumscribe it so that they are not bound to create 'mono-technic' institutions like the ones we have at present. It should be open to the Secretary of State or a local authority to propose to train teachers in polytechnic institutions.

While retaining the central power of initiative in the hands of the Secretary of State, it would seem appropriate to recast the regulations on the training of teachers to give local authorities and colleges more independence. It should surely be possible to make the Training of Teachers Regulations look very like the new Further Education Regulations, which are couched in the most general terms. Lest anyone in the Department should feel that the educational level of the colleges would immediately decline, the Secretary of State could be given the same sort of power of approval of courses as exists for advanced courses in further education. But it does not seem at all necessary that the Secretary of State should have to lay down such detail as the duration of courses and entry qualifications of students.

Colleges of education should continue to be administered (as are colleges of further education) by the local education authorities or voluntary bodies. As a consequence of the *Weaver Report* and the Education (No. 2) Act, 1968, the government of colleges has been greatly liberalized. The liberalization has gone nowhere near far enough, even in theory. In practice, many local authorities are far from implementing the letter, let alone the spirit, of the new legislation.

On the other hand, administration by local authorities is essential because of the need to link colleges of education more formally with polytechnics and other technical colleges. In some localities this will be easy. Indeed in two places a college of education has become part of a polytechnic, and there are five polytechnics with departments of education. But the process could go a great deal further. Where colleges of education exist in or near the centres of towns or cities, an administrative link with near-by colleges of further education might relatively easily be arranged.

It is more difficult to suggest tidy administrative solutions for those colleges in remote rural retreats. On the other hand, the logic of the policy outlined in this chapter is that teachers should cease to be trained in such isolated institutions: over the years their buildings should be converted to some other purpose. The most obvious might be the in-service training of teachers, where the idea of a 'retreat' could have positive advantages. Meanwhile, the remote colleges could continue to be administered by their local authorities or by the voluntary bodies which established them.

Administration, however, is only half the difficulty. There remains the problem of academic oversight, and again the logic of this chapter is that this question should be thought out again from the beginning. The experience in teacher education during the last twenty-five years suggests very strongly that the academic links between the colleges and universities have been a mistake: they have contributed to the difficulties which they were designed to avoid. It is time to return to something like the proposal put forward by the minority on the McNair Committee. Of course, in those days the particular proposal may have seemed unconvincing, because the only device available for academic oversight was the joint board, somewhat on the analogy of those boards set up to administer the National Certificate and Diploma schemes. It may well have been argued that such a body was not appropriate, and even if one does not accept this it is easy to understand that it may have been unappealing to teachers in the colleges. But the last fifteen years have seen the development of an institution whose use in this context would be entirely appropriate. It is the Council for National Academic Awards. This body, which validates degree-level courses in colleges of further education and awards degrees on the successful completion of them, has recently been extending its activities beyond those of its predecessor, the National Council for Technological Awards, and particularly into the social sciences. A college of education, forming part of a polytechnic, would then very reasonably submit its proposals for degree and other courses to the same body which was validating the other courses in the college. This arrangement would have several evident advantages. In the first place teacher education would have a national validation of its standards which it lacks at present. Second, it would be carried on in institutions where it was recognized as an equal with other disciplines. Third, it would share fully in the life of an academic community in both administrative and academic terms. Fourth, it would derive from the CNAA the opportunity to develop sandwich courses and to innovate in other ways which is largely absent through the university connection. In short, the arguments against the public control of teacher-training colleges, which derived largely from the need to assure them a respectable academic connection, no longer apply. In academic terms there is an obvious alternative to the oversight of universities, and there can be no ground, now, for not taking it.

There are other advantages too, of which the chief is the possibility of creating degree-level courses which relate to social work generally but which have in them the possibility of preparation for teaching. This kind of flexibility is impossible at present largely because of the rigid departmentalism of academic life. Much of what teachers want from their education can be obtained through the flexible possibilities offered by the CNAA.

What has been outlined here is not a guarantee of reform in teacher education. The most that can be claimed is that it will remove some of the bugbears and make rational teacher education more likely. It is an administrative structure which will make easier the growth of a fully professional teacher education at degree level. Its influence on the schools, and on higher education as a whole, could be profound.

References

1. T. Burgess and J. Pratt, *Policy and Practice: The Colleges of Advanced Technology*, Allen Lane The Penguin Press, 1970.
2. *Ninth Report of the National Advisory Council on the Training and Supply of Teachers*, HMSO, May 1965.

8 The Government of Colleges of Education
Terence A. Lockett

The colleges of education are 'the servants of three masters', namely, the Department of Education and Science, the local education authorities and the universities. The manner in which these three elements have exercised their control has changed considerably during the past decade and still continues to change. This complexity of external control tends to inhibit the freedom of college internal self-government. The primary concern of this chapter is with the *internal* government of the colleges; with the developments of the past decade and the possibilities for the future. The consequences of serving three masters will be manifest throughout.

College government in the 1960s
At the opening of the decade most colleges were relatively small. College government was mainly in the hands of the principal, who resembled an absolute monarch, unhampered by representative institutions. In the small colleges this system could, and often did, work reasonably well, depending on the character and ability of the principal. He could easily meet his entire staff and discuss college policy, or he could rely upon a few chosen advisers. There were also those who did not share their thoughts with the staff, who discouraged discussion and who took refuge in confidentiality.

As early as 1958 the Council of the ATCDE passed a resolution affirming

... that this Council considers that the time has long passed when the academic policy of a college could properly be determined by a governing body, or by a principal without the fullest consultation of the college's academic staff, and urges that each college should have a properly constituted academic board with rules of procedure determined by that board and with provision for democratic discussion and decision, including the right to vote, on academic matters.

This demand for staff participation in policy formulation and decision making was met in some colleges; in a great many others there was no response.

The lengthening of the training course from two to three years brought with it an influx of tutors from the schools in the autumn of 1962. In one stride most common rooms experienced a 40 to 50 per cent increase in their numbers. Many of these newcomers were young men and women from grammar and comprehensive schools whose chief concern was the teaching of their subject. To some the enclosed, paternalistic world of the training college came as a shock. The issues were important, but they were never debated. The schools from which they had just emerged were developing a liberality of outlook which contrasted markedly with the hierarchically structured college system. A renewed impetus was given to the ATCDE resolution, but no formal steps were taken.

In 1963 the Committee on Higher Education under the chairmanship of Lord Robbins recommended that training colleges should become part of the university structure, financed through the University Grants Committee. In rejecting this at the end of 1964, the Government announced the establishment of a study group on the government of colleges of education under the chairmanship of T. R. Weaver of the Department of Education and Science. The purpose of the study group was expressed in its report[1]: 'Our purpose throughout has been to enable the colleges to take full academic responsibility and to exercise it in an atmosphere of freedom, unhindered by unnecessary restrictions.' The membership of the group was drawn from the local authorities, the voluntary (religious) bodies, and the universities and staffs of the colleges represented by their professional organization, the ATCDE.

The report's main recommendations were framed to achieve the purpose quoted above, and in three areas were of particular importance:

We therefore recommend that the Secretary of State should introduce legislation to provide for the making by local education authorities of instruments of government for the constitution of the governing bodies of maintained colleges and to provide that these colleges should be conducted in accordance with articles of government made by an order of the local education authority and approved by him[2].

This recommendation sought to secure governing bodies on which representatives of the universities, of college academic staff and of 'persons with a concern for teacher training or specialist subjects' would be present in substantial numbers. There was also a strong hint that 'persons representing the authorities' need not necessarily form a majority on reconstituted governing bodies. Concerning the internal government of the colleges, the study group recommended 'as essential that every college should have a properly constituted academic board'. The board should consist of from twelve to twenty-five members, drawn from three categories: principal lecturers with responsibility allowances, representatives of departments not included in the first category, and a third group of members 'elected by the teaching staff as a whole'. Finally, 'to encourage as much delegation as possible by authorities to their colleges', a senior administrative officer (SAO) should be appointed in each college; 'he would be a member of the college staff and owe his allegiance to the governing body, to whom he would be administratively responsible through the principal'. He would also act as clerk to the governing body and be responsible under the direction of the principal for preparation of the estimates of expenditure and for general administration and maintenance.

These three recommendations caused considerable dispute. The main areas of conflict – the composition of the governing body, especially the LEAs' majority and the full voting membership of academic staff, the position of the SAO, and the governing body's relations with the LEA, particularly over finance – divided the Association of Municipal Corporations and the County Councils Associations, on the one hand, from the ATCDE, firmly supported by the universities, on the other. As the argument developed both the comparative innocence of college staff as to how they were governed and the complexities of local government were painfully revealed. Principals struggled with detailed arguments about the status of governing bodies as subcommittees of further education subcommittees which were themselves subcommittees of the education committee, which in turn had to heed decisions of establishment subcommittees made at the behest of the finance committee and subject to the approval of city or county council. Rarely can academics have endured such a concentrated and crucial series of political lessons.

Also actively engaged was the DES, which in February 1967 sent out *Circular 2/67*. This requested the LEAs to inform the Secretary of State of the action they had taken to reconstitute the governing bodies of their colleges and to submit draft articles of government for his approval. (Similar action was taken regarding the voluntary colleges.) This circular was followed in March by a *Model Scheme of Government for Voluntary Colleges* and in April by *Administrative Memorandum No. 8/67 Polytechnics*. Both these documents postulated forms of government for the respective bodies which were close to the Weaver pattern. Significantly, the LEAs were informed, in effect, that they could not have their polytechnics if they did not agree to establish a Weaver form of government. This was crucial. The intervention of the DES at this stage was a salutary reminder to the LEAs of what was required of them. Nevertheless, college staff and the ATCDE continued to be alarmed, and often with good reason. Schemes submitted to the Secretary of State in response to *Circular 2/67* often did not provide for representation of academic staff on governing bodies (or denied them voting rights), and frequently the senior administrative officer was not designated clerk to the governors. Financial arrangements were also most unsatisfactory in many cases. Clearly more pressure was needed to force the recalcitrant authorities to recognize that the colleges were national academic institutions of higher education and not simply post-secondary schools belonging to their own area (indeed many authorities had identical regulations governing their colleges and their secondary schools).

In March 1967 a further contestant appeared – the National Union of Students. On 21 March the Union published *Representation, Discipline and Autonomy*. The document presented a reasoned case for student participation in various areas of university and college life. A key statement, in the present context, was: 'We wish, then, to see provision for student repre-

sentation on the governing bodies and academic boards of
institutions written into the articles of government or into the
charter.' By many academics this request was dismissed as
hare-brained, impractical and even absurd. Less than four years
later the document appears reasonable, tentative and even conservative. Whatever else it may have been, it was not ineffective.

By November 1967 a Bill had been drawn up and introduced
into the House of Lords. The details of the parliamentary
struggle need not concern us here. In its original form the Bill
did not require LEAs to submit instruments of government for
the approval of the Secretary of State. This was crucial, as it is in
the instrument that the composition and powers of the governing body are delineated. It was thus open to the more conservative LEAs to evade the spirit of the *Weaver Report* and establish
governing bodies on which academic staff were not properly represented or did not have full voting powers. In fact, the LEAs
had made it clear that submission of the instrument 'would
impugn the competence of the local education authorities and
. . . reopen the whole question of their acceptance of the *Weaver
Report* as a whole'. The rearguard action was still very strong.
Thus, despite excellent advocacy by Lord Aberdare in the Lords
and Sir Edward (now Lord) Boyle and other MPs in the Commons, it appeared that the LEAs would have their way. Even
the ATCDE appears to have believed the cause was lost and
to have settled for an unamended Bill.

However, possibly as a result of student pressure, or unofficial representations by interested MPs, or more likely through
renewed civil-service pressure on ministers, and steadfast university opinion, the Government's resolution stiffened. The
LEAs gave way. In the third reading in the Commons, Mrs
Shirley Williams, the Minister of State, announced that the Bill
was to be amended in a manner which gave the Secretary of
State the right to approve the instrument, and thus to ensure
that the body of governors constituted thereunder met with
his approval. The colleges could claim to have won. The Bill
received its third reading on 9 May 1968.

Subsequently the LEAs have had to frame fresh instruments
and articles. For some, this was the second time in two years,
and in one local authority no fewer than eleven separate drafts

have been submitted to colleges for their comments over the past four years. To complete the historical record it should be added that when the model instruments and articles for polytechnics were produced they incorporated many of the points which were still at issue in some of the colleges. This was particularly the case in relation to student representation on governing bodies and academic boards (a matter not dealt with by the Weaver study group); the composition of the governors; the position of the SAO; and the making of liberal financial arrangements. The LEAs were now forced to grant to the colleges and to the students the same rights which had been granted to staff and students in the polytechnics. If they did not, the Secretary of State would reject the proposed instruments and articles.

In this very real political struggle of the past few years many elements have played their part. They range from the staff of colleges bargaining with their own local education authority, and through the ATCDE at national level, to the MPs and university vice-chancellors who have consistently upheld the Weaver line. More than academic freedom has been at stake. The struggle has been for power and control. Not absolute power or total control, but that reasonable and responsible freedom from the irritating oversight of local bureaucracy, which can create the environment for the healthy growth and development of an academic community. It is a tangled story and one that reflects little credit on many local authorities, as represented by their associations. At the same time it should be recorded that many elected councillors and LEA officials have been liberal and responsible. The principals and staff of some colleges were fully consulted by the officials who administered them; their views have been listened to sympathetically and acted upon. But many LEAs have not been as generous and forthcoming. Had it not been for the consistent support of the officials of the DES, of university opinion, of the pressure brought to bear through the polytechnics and the NUS leadership of the student case, the outcome almost certainly would have been different. It is to the credit of the Government and to the then chief Opposition spokesman on education, Lord Boyle, that the very substantial pressure for the dilution of the

Weaver Report brought to bear by the LEAs was ultimately resisted and rejected.

If this seems a complacent note upon which to end this section, let Lord Boyle have the last word: 'None of us believes that we have yet reached the last word with regard to either the future of the colleges or their relationship with the university system.'

The present position

Today the situation is one of change and adjustment to change. Academic boards should have been established in all colleges; new instruments and articles of government have come into operation; senior administrative officers have been appointed. Thus the full system of internal self-government envisaged by the Weaver study group should be the pattern in all colleges. Though for some institutions the element of change will be relatively small, in all colleges there will be areas which will demand an adjustment in attitudes and outlook. The time-lag between the *Weaver Report* and its implementation seemed interminable to many college lecturers, but to others subsequent developments – especially the presence of students on committees and academic boards – are still both strange and unwelcome. Many members of staff sit very uneasily in their committee room places, and many an LEA official and governor has found it difficult to adapt. Nor have some of the more conservative and authoritarian principals found their new roles very palatable. Old habits die hard. The future will not afford a universally easy passage. What are the chief problems? How will the colleges face their new responsibilities?

The *Weaver Report* recommended that academic boards should range in size from twelve to twenty-five. This was a reasonable number in 1966 when a college with a staff of over seventy-five was very much the exception. Today several colleges have staff of 125 to 160. The academic board in such colleges will have to be larger than envisaged by the study group, or it will fail to contain the recommended range of representation. Some colleges have already tried boards which do not include a representative of each subject offered (as many as twenty different subjects are taught in some of the larger colleges): subjects have been grouped together, either formally or informally, into faculties, and it is these which are represented on the board. The number of students eligible is also contentious. Some boards have as many as ten student members; in others only the president of the students' union, and perhaps one other, has a seat.

There is no 'right' number or combination for the composition of an academic board, but one on which fewer than one-sixth of the total staff have seats is in danger of becoming a close-knit oligarchy. In a large college with many departments, with a reasonable proportion of elected members (say 25 per cent of staff membership) and a fair student representation, the board could easily total forty or more. Experience alone will indicate at what point such a large body ceases to work effectively. Whatever the size of the board, the need to think out its procedures and a sound committee structure may be hard for lecturers unfamiliar with political forms. They are unused to participating in the democratic government of an institution through committee work. If they have been in colleges for any length of time, they will no doubt have served under an 'absolute monarch' type of principal and the political processes of policy formation and decision making will not be a part of their normal mode of working. It will be some time before this form of activity is integrated into the routine.

Under the articles of government the college academic board has responsibility for certain areas of college life. On paper these appear to be liberal and far-ranging, especially if viewed in the perspective of the pre-Weaver structure. Primarily, the academic board is responsible for 'the academic work of the college and reviewing methods of teaching'. The exercise of this responsibility is not as straightforward as it may appear. Let us presume that within a college there is widespread support for a one-year foundation course of 'integrated study'. The idea has been canvassed amongst the students through departmental staff–student committees, and welcomed. Preliminary work has been done in academic board committees, and agreement secured from departments with a strong vested interest in the *status quo*. The academic board has passed a formal resolution accepting as college policy the establishment of an integrated foundation course for all first-year students. If we also presume that the governors have been informed and have raised no objections, it would seem that the way ahead is clear. But at this point the external controls are encountered. To secure the reform each subject will have to obtain the approval or acquiescence of the appropriate board of study of the ATO. There may well be resistance and refusal at this level. At the next stage the professional board will ask: will the course be examined? By what methods? What organ of the School of Education and the university in general is to oversee course content? Just as some LEAs are more flexible than others, so some ATOs more readily permit individual colleges to experiment than others. The example chosen is a normal routine type of change, and most colleges would meet sufficient goodwill to enable them to accomplish it. Others would not – so what has become of the academic freedom associated with the phrase 'having responsibility for the academic work of the college'? Such issues arise because this phrase is amenable to different interpretations. It is not that colleges seek total and irresponsible freedom from external control, but that within an agreed, generous and liberal framework, their freedom of action should be compatible with their status in the nation's higher education.

The academic board is also responsible for the admission, assessment and exclusion (for poor performance) of students. In this area there is perhaps less scope for conflict, though the 'type' of student who is acceptable to the college may be the subject of heated debate. But again, if we look outside the college, we find its freedom on admissions policy severely circumscribed by the DES. Total student numbers are prescribed by the Department; so, too, is the school age range for which the college may prepare its students. The DES is acutely concerned with teacher supply; with getting the right number of students, of the right sex, with the right training, to fit the known or projected needs of the schools. Maybe this is what the nation wants it to do. Perhaps college staffs are too introverted and forget their function – to educate the teachers of the nation's children. But the rigidity of approach and the secrecy and lack of consultation certainly limit the freedom of a board on admissions policy.

The board is also responsible for the arrangement of teaching practice and other practical training. The inhibiting factors here are the needs and expressed wishes of the schools which can limit experiment and the adoption of new methods. This may be frustrating for the innovators, but it is understandable that headteachers have no taste for their schools and children to be experiment fodder.

A vital role of the academic board concerns staffing: 'recommending the apportionment of the total number of teaching staff of different grades to departments and subjects'. Boards will have to form policy on new departments, on the amalgamation of existing departments, on the appointment to competing departments of scarce additional staff, and on recommending promotions. The articles of some colleges specify that promotion or appointment at principal-lecturer level shall be the responsibility of the governors; promotion at a lower level, to senior lecturer, shall be on the recommendation of the principal advised by the staff. In some colleges both the allocation of new appointments or replacements and staff promotions are discussed in full board meetings. Many colleges, however, delegate the main work of promotion and appointment to a small staffing committee. The matter is sensitive because the future of departments and individuals is at stake, and because in the past it was almost the private preserve of the principal. Many principals are reluctant to share it even with senior staff, and are supported by colleagues who feel that here a single person is better than a committee. The reluctance to discuss and evaluate the merits of a colleague or of his department, and the obvious desire to evade the responsibility and place it in the hands of one who is alleged to be 'paid to do it', could inhibit the development of responsible self-government. It is an example of avoiding the real issues, to which reference has been made elsewhere in this book.

Finance is another responsibility the academic board now shares which some tutors would prefer to be without. The SAO is responsible for the preparation of the estimates, and the principal for their submission to governors. The board is charged with the duty of consultation. Library facilities, books, furniture, stationery, educational materials, educational visits and travel allowances, salaries (in the relevant sense of 'number and grades to different departments'), the establishment of technical, clerical and ancillary staff, and a host of smaller matters may all be reviewed by the board before the estimates are submitted. Finance has always held something of a mystery for most college tutors, who are reluctant to scrutinize the estimates of colleagues with any thoroughness.

Finally, very considerable changes have taken place recently in college discipline and staff–student relations. Articles of government now contain provision for joint disciplinary committees composed of equal numbers of staff and students. In many colleges these committees have not long been formed and their effectiveness is as yet unknown, though clearly they will help to create a better climate. On the more general question of staff–student relationships, student membership of departmental committees, academic boards and governing bodies has helped to dilute some of the cruder authoritarian elements in the 'we–them' confrontation. Since the lowering of the age of majority to eighteen, staff are no longer in *loco parentis*. The consequences of this are still not fully comprehended by staff or students.

No academic board can properly cope with all its areas of responsibility unless it is prepared to discuss policy at least once a week *or* is willing to establish a properly structured committee system. Already many colleges have realized the futility of setting up *ad hoc* committees and working parties as the need arose, and have organized a workable committee system. The simplest pattern is to match the standing committees of the board to the functions as prescribed in the articles. This would give a range of committees for: academic matters (which in a large college would need several subcommittees to deal separately with B.Ed., Certificate and curriculum courses), admissions and records, teaching practice, staffing, finance, discipline, educational resources (for library, visual educational material and courses, closed-circuit TV, etc.). There needs to be a staff–student council for the discussion of general college relations and, lastly, a general purposes committee to act as a procedure committee for the academic board (to be 'keeper of the constitution') and to act as 'sweeper-up' on general matters such as college premises, international exchanges, conferences and kindred matters. Each college will differ in its approach, but two points are fundamental. The first is that students are full members of all those committees to which they can contribute. In the committee structure outlined, the only committee from which students would be excluded is the staffing committee, though their usefulness on the finance committee might also be questioned. Second, a network of committees implies staff participation at all levels. Much committee work could best be done by tutors not on the academic board. It is implicit also in this outline that the committees exist to help the board. Issues should have been fully debated in committee and an agreed policy presented to the board for its approval or rejection. The bulk of the board's work would be the receiving of reports from the standing committees and taking appropriate action after reasonably short debate. This does not imply automatic 'rubber stamping' or the exclusion of urgent business which might be fully debated initially in the board, but it does imply the acceptance of some responsibility for policy formulation in specific areas by the majority of the academic staff.

It must be admitted that if anyone has lost authority and power as a result of the *Weaver Report*, it is the principal. It is too much to say that he has declined from being the visible and absolute source of authority within the college to the humbler station as 'chairman of colleagues'. But the 'new model' principal has a difficult and somewhat ambiguous role. He can no longer make academic policy unilaterally. Circumstances often render this difficult, for there is a continuous dialogue between college principals and chief education officers; and less frequently, but no less importantly, between the DES and principals. It requires considerable restraint for the principal to avoid committing the college to a course of action, and to answer: 'I shall have to put this before my academic board.' For some, particularly (but not necessarily) those who held office before the *Weaver Report*, this requires a difficult adjustment, and not all have made it successfully.

The principal's power has also been limited by the inclusion of academic staff and students on governing bodies. In the past principals have returned from governors' meetings with scarcely concealed delight to inform tutors' meetings (or academic boards) that the governors have rejected a particular scheme. 'I did what I could on your behalf, but I must say that I agreed with some of the governors' objections. As it stood the scheme was unworkable.' With some such bland platitude a promising reform was stifled. Now this infuriating type of sabotage is less likely.

A further way in which the principal may seek to retain control is by setting up rival organizations like heads of departments' or tutors' meetings. A skilful principal can so manipulate a heads-of-department meeting that it emasculates the academic board, and returns to him a measure of personal control. This may reflect a subconscious hankering after the old way of working with a few senior colleagues, more than any outright Machiavellianism. What, then, should be the role of the 'new model' principal? In academic matters it is his function – with other college officials – to implement the policy of the board. He is not chief legislator but he remains chief executive. He also retains very wide powers under the articles which normally specify 'that subject to other provisions contained herein, the principal shall be responsible to the governors for the internal organization, management and discipline of the college, and shall exercise supervision over the academic and non-academic staff'. This is open to interpretations, but the wise principal will refrain from quoting this article on every occasion when he is not getting his own way!

The principal will also represent the college at many levels: delegacy, the professional board, the faculty, the School or Institute of Education, and in day-to-day contact with the CEO and the DES. To most of these meetings he will go armed with college opinion as expressed at academic board meetings. If on occasion he is advancing a policy with which he has only limited sympathy, it is still his duty to represent it as forcefully as he can, even though he may find it embarrassing and even distasteful.

With the appointment of the SAO, most principals have fewer routine tasks. Committee work may consume much of this saved time, but a principal should be able to find more for educational themes, long-term thinking, maintaining contacts with the DES, with his fellow principals in the ATO and through

the ATCDE, and attending professional courses and conferences. This reading, thinking and talking should be shared with
his colleagues. If they are immersed in their teaching, reading,
marking, researching and school visiting, the principal can direct
their attention to developments in teacher education, and make
them aware of research and experiment, so that the quality of
teaching and methods of work within the college are constantly
under review.

The 'new' principal will have shed the paternalistic, monarchi-
cal role. He needs far more skill, intelligence and diplomacy,
much greater stamina and powers of persuasion, than did his
predecessors. Held less in awe and more easy of access, responsible for much larger staffs and more plant and equipment, with
adults as students, with tensions and conflicts more open, the
qualities of mind and character demanded are greater than ever.
His crude power may have been diminished, but the liveliness
and harmony of the enlarged community still depend upon him.

Many colleges have only recently been able to appoint a
senior administrative officer. The voluntary colleges have for
some time enjoyed internal administration, but for the LEA
colleges this is a new experience. The present role of the SAO
is not entirely clear. Some LEAs appear to regard the SAO as
'their man in the college', though fortunately these seem to be
in the minority.

Finance and the control of estimates is central to the government of colleges and to the duties of the SAO. Under the
articles the SAO is responsible for drawing up the estimates,
and the principal, after consulting the academic board, presents
them to the governors. It is on financial matters that college–
LEA relationships have often been most strained. The central
issue is how to reconcile the principle of academic freedom
with public accountability. The LEAs who administer colleges
draw much of the necessary finance from 'the pool'. This is a
device to compensate authorities who run colleges for the
expense incurred, and all LEAs pay into the pool in proportion
to their school population figures[3]. The annual bargaining over
estimates before 1969 was most unsatisfactory. Now that
governing bodies are no longer subcommittees of subcommittees, their estimates go directly to the finance committee and

thence to the city or county council. Although some of the signs are ambiguous, there is considerable room for optimism over the working of the new arrangements. Once the estimates are finally approved, the college has much greater freedom of manoeuvre and, through the governors, much more freedom to exercise virement. But the global total given to colleges is still entirely at the discretion of the LEA, strongly pressed behind the scenes by the pooling committee. All the evidence here, especially in the light of recent Government statements, is that in real terms the colleges are on as tight a rein as ever. It is public money which is being spent and accountability is essential. There has, however, long been the feeling that the LEA attitude has been pinch-penny. This may be grossly unfair to some LEAs, but it is perhaps a reflection of resentment at the manner in which detailed supervision has been exercised by establishment and finance committees who, it seems, have acted upon a crude mathematical cost-effective basis with no consideration or understanding of the educational issues involved. The new system has placed day-to-day control within the colleges in the hands of the SAO. It still remains to be seen whether this will remove resentments, or whether the LEAs will seek to interfere, possibly as agents of the pooling committee, in a manner which goes beyond the bounds of securing reasonable public accountability.

Finally, as the DES still controls the general size and character of the colleges, and itself often operates through the agency of the pooling committee, the really crucial decisions (and it may be argued that in the national interest this is rightly so) are taken at a level well above that of the college academic board. The new-found freedom in formulating academic policy is severely circumscribed by all these factors which, along with the 'freedoms', are enshrined in the articles:

The college shall be conducted in accordance with the provisions of the Education Act, 1944, as amended by any subsequent enactment, and any Regulations made thereunder and with the Regulations of the Area Training Organization of which the college is a member and with these Articles.

The local education authority after consultation with the governors shall be responsible, within any limits specified by the

Secretary of State for Education and Science, for determining the
educational character of the college, and its place in the educational
system.

Freedom is very relative!

The structure as outlined here may appear complex, even
cumbersome. It would perhaps be instructive to look briefly at
a case which serves to highlight the strengths and weaknesses
of the new system. *College Letter 16/69* was sent out by the
DES in September 1969 to the clerks of the governing bodies
of voluntary colleges. Its principal concern was 'the possibility
of establishing norms for particular items of expenditure', with
special reference to teaching staff costs. This was to be achieved
by a standardization in staff–student ratios. It was suggested
that the staff–student ratio bands in all colleges should be:

Number of students	Ratio band	Mid-ratio
Under 350	9·4–11·0	10·2
350–549	9·9–11·1	10·5
550 and over	10·1–11·3	10·7

College Letter 16/69 was also sent to chief education officers
whose LEAs maintained colleges. It was recommended that
colleges with more favourable staff–student ratios should make
the necessary adjustments over a three-year period. How have
colleges in this position reacted, given the present system of
government? In many cases the principal initially reported the
letter to the staff as a whole. Subsequently, discussions have
been held at departmental level, by faculties, by meetings of the
whole academic staff, by the staffing committee of the academic
board, and by the full board. Colleges have prepared a strategy
which has been presented to governors for their approval, and
finance committees, education committees, LEA officials and
the DES have all contributed to the debate. All the elements
in the government of colleges have been brought into play. A
great deal of time has been consumed. Many will ask, could it
not all have been settled in ten minutes by the principal's undertaking to reduce his staff by two each year for the next three
years? Of course it could. That is how it would have been done

in many colleges before the *Weaver Report*. College self-government is time-consuming and many academic staff believe that
they have better things to do. It is their right not to participate.
But the opportunity is there and the prospects of a mutually
satisfactory solution are greater from consultation than from
arbitrary pronouncements. This is the justification for the internal self-government of an academic community. It is not an
end in itself. It is the most promising method we have devised
for creating the best environment in which to perform our
major task – the education and training of teachers.

The future

The structure of college government given in this chapter will
not always work. Colleges differ, academic staff differ and so
do principals and students. Nor will the structure which suits a
city college for mature day students preoccupied with professional training be acceptable, or desirable, in a large, rural,
residential college which prides itself upon its academic standards. In this sense the *Weaver Report* is 'the end of the beginning'. It is possible to isolate four potential or actual sources of
weakness.

First, there is the recalcitrant principal, who interprets the
articles illiberally, who takes decisions on academic policy
unilaterally, or who cannot reconcile himself to his role: the
sort of person who caused one exasperated board member to
interrupt a lofty monologue with: 'What is the point of having
an academic board when all we do is listen whilst you tell us
what you are going to do?'

Second, there is the unwillingness of many staff to participate.
'We haven't the time to waste in committee work', 'Let's get on
with the real job' are sentiments frequently expressed. People
cannot be forced to participate, and any individual tutor can
decide not to forsake his teaching or research for the political
battles of the board room. But non-participants should realize
that they are surrendering a right, and that actions which they
abhor may be as much the consequence of their 'opting-out' as
of those who have legislated in their absence.

A third threat is posed by over-zealous reformers. Mainly
because they are 'ideas-men' and deeply involved in internal

political activity, they tend to repel and alienate both the non-participants and the more conservative elements. They become labelled 'careerists' and 'opportunists'. For them the present is never right. Constant change is the only equilibrium they can contemplate. They are as intolerant of the ideas and values of others, as they are positive of the rightness of their own current obsession. Yet it is often from this body of radicalism that most of the dynamic and creative policies in the college emerge. The problem for the principal – always presuming he is not the chief radical – is to prevent the academic board from degenerating into a set-piece conflict between the radicals and the conservatives. If 'consensus' is the lowest common denominator to be avoided at all costs, what is the alternative? Creative conflict? ('All conflict creates is ulcers', was a recently heard common-sense remark.) Or creative cooperation? If this is any different from consensus, how is it to be achieved? Is it too pious to echo the words of the *Weaver Report* that tensions 'can be relaxed and most of them can be removed by patient and frank discussion and the exercise of goodwill ...'? If they cannot and colleges fail to exercise self-government responsibly, their future independence is endangered.

The final weakness is a consequence of serving three masters. The present structure is cumbersome and needs reform. Nobody advocates the removal of external accountability for expenditure. Colleges must also be accountable for the level, quality and relevance of the courses they offer as initial or further training for teachers. Is the present structure the best means of ensuring this accountability? Most college staff are positive that it is not. Through the ATCDE, pressure has been exerted for many years to remove colleges from LEA financial control and place them, as Robbins recommended, both academically and financially, under the universities. Their status would in this view be enhanced as 'liberal arts' colleges offering courses other than those directly related to teacher education. Others support 'polyversities' or advocate a comprehensive system of higher education. On the other hand, the LEAs will not lightly abandon their connection with the colleges and are curiously – in the light of recent history – finding growing support from many college lecturers. The latter doubt the wisdom of merging with the universities, whose conservative and restrictive thinking they fear. They note the low esteem in which 'education' is held. Many believe that the colleges are in real danger of losing those aspects of self-government so recently and so difficultly won. For those who think in these terms, the solution lies in the polytechnic structure, internal administration and academic self-government, a financial relationship with a reorganized local-government unit, and an academic relationship with the CNAA.

What the colleges want to emerge from Lord James's inquiry is a clear indication that the status of teacher education is to be enhanced and not diminished. The future administrative structure should be such as to render this more, not less, likely. The measure of internal self-government and administration already secured should be developed and increased. Finally, responsibility for the pattern of teacher education should rest in the hands of those best qualified to exercise it – educators, college staffs, students and teachers.

References

1. *Report of the Study Group on the Government of Colleges of Education* (*Weaver Report*), HMSO, 1966, para. 9.

2. *Report of the Study Group on the Government of Colleges of Education* (*Weaver Report*), HMSO, 1966, para. 107.

3. Department of Education and Science, *Report on Education*, no. 43, 1968.

Prospect: School in the 1980s
Harry Rée

We shouldn't train soldiers to fight the last war; nor should we train teachers to work in yesterday's schools. Tomorrow's schools are going to be very different from schools we have ever known. This chapter projects a model of what they might be like; it is based partly on what is already happening in a few forward-looking schools, and partly on the hopes and aspirations of students and young teachers who will probably be heads or hold other posts at the top of the education ladder in fifteen or twenty years' time. The children in these schools will be different; so will the teachers. In preparing teachers for the schools of tomorrow, it's important to have an idea of what these schools will be like.

The railings have gone for scrap; the hedges are one foot high; there are no gates to shut. Inside the buildings the teachers have left their platforms; they are working at desks, moving around, attending meetings, taking tutorials. If there are doors they are often open, and the walls can be replaced or removed with ease. The school isn't under one roof; it's dispersed among and between this cluster of buildings which the community has provided for itself.* Everyone comes here: pregnant mothers come to the clinic for a check-up, mothers leave their toddlers at the playgroup, while they go to work or attend a class or meeting in near-by rooms. Old-age pensioners come to their club in the afternoons. In the evenings young couples and

* It is significant that in *Circular 2/70* (2 February 1970) the DES advised local education authorities to negotiate with other local authorities and with other departments of their own authority, and with the relevant voluntary associations, with a view to establishing on one site community schools which would offer a multitude of social, recreational and educational opportunities, normally provided in separate buildings or on separate sites, and often by separate departments. The motive behind this was explicitly stated as being 'to obtain better value for money'.

spinsters, teenagers and bachelors come to attend courses, to go dancing or swimming. There are halls, lounges and libraries, there are seminar rooms, workshops and laboratories, a restaurant and a bar, a self-service store and a citizens' advice bureau; there are games fields, squash courts, a youth wing, a medical room and a gym. Most of the floors are carpeted, and most of the rooms have comfortable chairs. The reading room is quiet, but there's a smaller and even quieter room, with pictures and sculpture on view. Some of the rooms will be used by children only; some by adults only; a great many by both. At weekends there is usually a wedding reception, and often private parties go on in the evenings. School has regained its original Greek meaning: a place for worthwhile leisure.

In the daytime it's mostly children who occupy the buildings. The young ones are usually grouped with their own teacher. They are working usually in small groups, often helped by 'aides', trained adults who can supplement the teacher, taking responsibility, under supervision, for small groups, and attending to the incessant demands of the smaller children. There will be some special lessons taken by specialist teachers – a short foreign-language session once a day, extra maths, remedial reading. Secondary students are increasingly expected to organize their own time, after having been assigned work by different specialist teachers and tutors; this may involve working on their own or in groups of four or five; they will work from books or cards or tapes extracted from the library or from the school resource unit – this is kept stocked and up to date by the regional teachers' centre. At set times they will come together for a special lecture or a carefully selected film; at set times they will move into their seminar groups for free or guided discussions; sometimes they will have tutorials when their assignment work and their essays will be discussed and assessed. Outside these times they are free to come or go; some stay in the library, some go home and work; some go into the town.

At the beginning of each term all students will have had a private session with their tutors, and agreed the courses they will follow. These will be balanced between what must be done to achieve certain qualifications relevant to the individual's aspirations, and what will be done for pure interest and fun, there is of course no reason why the two should not coincide. Each student will have a record card on which will be indicated his various assignments, and details of the compulsory contact periods with staff. Tutors will enter their marks, assessments and tutorial comments in a special column. Students will not be confined to the school during the day, but they may well be found there during the evening, perhaps joining teachers and other adults on courses, or in handicraft classes, attending political meetings or concerts, or just relaxing, eating and drinking with friends and neighbours, or even parents.

The LEA has provided the school, but it is governed by an elected Assembly which meets in open session once a term, and represents all users – teachers, parents, students, as well as councillors. A governing body, acting as an executive committee of the Assembly, is formed from the members. The head is ex officio a member of the governors. When he resigns or retires the governing body appoints his successor. The present head started his career as a teacher, became a head of department, then the curriculum organizer in a big high school; while doing this he was appointed part-time tutor to education students at a near-by polytechnic, who were preparing for the General Teaching Certificate. This kept him in touch with ideas current in the education department, and allowed him to supervise in his own school the teaching practice of a number of students. At the age of forty-two he took a term off to attend a course in school administration, and shortly afterwards was appointed head of the community college. Under him, and also appointed by the governing body, are four special deputies. One is responsible for the junior department of the school. Another is concerned with curriculum planning in the whole school for the full-time students between thirteen and eighteen years of age. A third is responsible for coordinating house activities, such as counselling, careers advice and home–school relations. He is the chairman of the houses committee; there are five houses, each with a head and deputy. There are three hundred students in each house. The fourth deputy is responsible for the post-school activities, dealing therefore with the Youth Wing, the adult classes, and all the other evening and weekend activities. (He also teaches some French in the school, which keeps him in touch with the staffroom.)

The heads of department in the school work closely with the curriculum organizer, who can thus coordinate new plans and keep information flowing across the departmental gaps. Some of the heads of departments are closely involved, as part-time tutors attached to the local polytechnic or college of education, in teacher training. They take student seminars, both at school and in the college or polytechnic, and supervise the work of students on practice and of teachers on probation who are attached to the school. Those who do this receive additional responsibility allowances.

More than half of the staff consists of teachers who have not only done their initial training and been awarded their General Teaching Certificate, but who have done, either concurrently with their initial-training course, or afterwards while in service, some course to qualify them to take on special responsibility in the school, perhaps as head of a department, or head of house, or in some particular field such as sports or drama. The school day, for teachers, no longer consists of seven or eight forty-minute slots, during which thirty or more children have to be taught. A teacher may well spend part of a morning with three colleagues and six students planning a course for the second half of the term. It may start, they'll decide, with a film or a lecture by a young teacher, or by an outsider. They'll be catering for a total of ninety students; after the first lecture these will be split up into groups of ten for discussions and distribution of assignments. Everyone, students and staff, is given a list of relevant books and articles available in the school library and resource unit. The student teachers taking seminars are supported by their head of department, who will drop in on the discussions with their groups, and offer advice. For the rest of the morning the student teachers may be free to prepare work, but the staff will find themselves seeing groups of three or four students at a time, for half an hour, discussing work, suggesting reading and visits, films to see, and written work to be done. Lunch is taken in the canteen by some children; others go to the town. In either case it's quite likely they'll not be eating with teachers, but with friends connected with school, perhaps as library supervisors, parents who are qualified swimming instructors, or maybe a policeman who has come in to give a talk. Some children are eating their sandwiches outside, or they may be sitting at lunch with teachers who have been taking them the previous period for a tutorial, or with a group of friends who left recently and who have come back to listen to a lunchtime disco. Some are working in the library at their assignments due next session. In the afternoon some of the teachers may be off duty, but they'll be on again in the evening, taking an adult class. Others may have quite normal lessons to give, in normal subjects (there is never total renewal).

But the children have changed. How? And in what way are the teachers different? And finally, in what way do the training and preparation of these teachers differ from the familiar pattern of department and college courses of former days? As far as the children are concerned, the new system of teaching and learning has not only had the expected educational consequences, but has brought with it social changes too. We had come to accept peer-group pressures as a paramount influence during adolescence, but the new system has begun to weaken this. No longer taught always in a class, every lesson with the same group, the child is much freer than before to strike out on his own, freed from the inordinate pressures of his classroom peers; and this process is carried further because of the possibility in the community school of meeting and associating, especially in the evenings, with adults other than teachers, and indeed with teachers who are increasingly becoming indistinguishable from other adults.

The teachers have joined a multifarious profession, where the jobs to be done in the school and in connection with the school are widely different in the demands they make, the qualifications required, and in the actual experience they offer. Teachers moreover don't expect to spend their whole career in school, their professional life is a series of variations on an educational theme, involving not only joint appointments (for example, the local authority music adviser, who serves also on the staff of a college) but also periods of secondment from the school to the Inspectorate or to administration, thus ensuring that good teachers move out of school but are not tempted permanently to stay away. And they are drawn back by good prospects – not only financial, but by prospects which don't limit them to standing in front of a class for most of their working week. But of course some may later move again, permanently, back into the field to which they had been seconded.

This change in teachers' experience has been matched by a change in what is expected of teachers by children, by parents and by society in general. In the days when teaching children was all done in classrooms in front of a single large group of thirty or more, and when the attempt had to be made to keep the whole group working at about the same pace, on the same subject, the first necessity, before the teacher could begin to teach, was the power to dominate and to control the squad. This necessity has begun to wither away, and the result has been magical; the school marm and the martinet have joined the dodo. With them have gone the shadow of dominant authority in which the children lived.

Contact between parents and teachers, the general public and teachers, has become far less formal and awkward; the attitude towards teachers has also changed; the uncertain mixture of awe and disparagement, left over partly from schooldays, has been largely replaced by feelings of mutual respect and friendliness, much more comparable to the feelings of a patient or his family towards their doctor; often the same social reactions will be expected of the teacher as we have traditionally expected of the doctor – approachability and indiscriminate concern. At the same time the professional style and the day-to-day life of the teacher has now come to resemble far more that of someone working in the modern university, where formal lectures have become much more rare than tutorials and seminars, and where students are expected to work on their own, without imminent or extraneous sanctions, and without threats of punishment held continuously over them. Finally, the expectation that teachers must be a special *genus*, undetachable from the little world of childhood and adolescence, and cloaked with a respectability that was little more than half human, has also disappeared. Thus the teacher is valued as highly as the private secretary, the accountant or the solicitor – and is equally difficult to recognize.

How and where are teachers trained for this new world? And for how long? And by whom? The traditional pattern of training has been broken and re-formed. Student teachers are no longer trapped at the end of a sixth-form course, for they share the initial stages of their training – of their tertiary education – not only with future social workers, but with young people who may be expecting to become architects, insurance clerks, accountants, or who simply have not yet made up their minds. And when the time comes for special professional courses to be taken, the student teachers are not directed into a special institution for themselves alone.

Courses and institutions vary in what they provide, and students can move, without much difficulty, from one to another. Auxiliary teachers can start earning after two years of training, which includes much practical experience. Normally, student teachers stay at least three years to achieve their General Teaching Certificate. This gives them the right to teach, but it would be rare for anyone holding only the GTC to be given any special responsibility. The pattern of the courses varies from institution to institution, some offering a much wider academic element than others, some offering the academic element mainly at the beginning of the course, others concurrently. One feature of training has become common; teachers have come to recognize that they needed to shoulder a much heavier share of the training burden than they have taken on in the recent past. This involved two changes. They had to insist that time and money should be provided for those teachers who took on this load; they had to agree that those who did so would have to be conversant with and not hostile to the current doctrines of the professional trainers of teachers. As a result, at least a half of the GTC course takes place in schools and is supervised by teachers who work partly as teachers under the authority of the school, and partly as trainers under the authority of the department or college. At the same time those working full time in the colleges or in the education departments of polytechnics or universities will often be seconded teachers, and often the school staffs will include a proportion of seconded trainers. Graduates who have not followed concurrent courses involving education will have had to take a two-year course to get the GTC, and in many departments this includes a four-term sandwich in schools.

A large number of teachers with the GTC are encouraged by pay and ambition to move on to positions of responsibility or special skill, but to do this they need to follow additional courses which may last one year, and which lead to fully qualified teacher status, with a commensurate increase in salary. Some of these courses can be taken part time, but most will demand some continuous study. They are designed with specific future responsibilities in mind, and each course will prepare teachers for a limited range of responsible jobs, both in schools and outside. Only these fully qualified teachers would be offered posts such as headships, head of a department, counsellor or housemaster; and the same fully qualified status would be necessary to join the Inspectorate or to supervise students in training.

The courses in all training institutions have been modified to allow for a large element of individual and group work, which matches the method which students are expected to practise when they get into schools. During the initial-training period the students will have become used to associating professionally with teachers and lecturers, and even with parents. They will have taken part in discussions about the planning of school courses and will have been expected to play an important part in the whole life of the school, extending into the evening and the weekend activities which, because they are open to the whole community, may have had little to do with teaching and teachers. Thus the school or schools where they have done their practice will have given them a taste for living in the wider community, the school has been seen as not a mere work place, visited between nine o'clock and four by conscripted children and salary-conscious adults, but a living collective, an open but inclusive community, with disparate activities and aims. These aims add up to one: to provide the opportunity for everyone in the neighbourhood to involve themselves, if they want to, in creation and re-creation. Through reading and discussion, through listening and performing, through study and through play the community school has become an educational generating station, preparing not only the child for a full life in the community, but offering parents and other adults a fuller share in life, and giving to aspirant teachers an opportunity to prepare themselves effectively both for their professional job and for living.

The picture projected above is not altogether fanciful. Schools something like the one imagined here are already operating, for example in Cumberland and Cambridgeshire. More sophisticated versions are emerging, for instance in Leicestershire and Nottinghamshire. Experiments in teaching practice for students already involve teams of them working under schoolteacher tutors, who receive pay for this extra work, for instance in Leicestershire and London. As far as the training and preparation of teachers is concerned action is of course required by the government, by universities, by colleges and polytechnics, by UCET, by the ATCDE, by the NUT and other teachers' associations, and not least by the local authorities. Is this too much to ask of an ageing England? We need to remind ourselves that education is wedded to the faith that the ideal and the actual can be made one – otherwise we flounder and perish.

Other Penguin Education Specials

The Impact of Robbins

Richard Layard, John King, Claus Moser

In 1963 the *Robbins Report* launched the most massive expansion of higher education ever seen in Britain. The aim was to create a new deal for the nation's talented young.

Yet today the chances of a sixth former getting a place at a British university are, if anything, slightly less than they were before the Report, and it is in the fields of teacher training and further education that the most significant expansions have taken place. Future trends point the same way.

Did Robbins succeed? Here the leaders of the team that did the research for that famous Report, Professor Claus Moser and Richard Layard, and their colleague at the London School of Economics, John King, look back over the past few years and explain what happened to the ambitious blueprint for creating a broader system of higher education in Britain.

Patterns and Policies in Higher Education

George Brosan, Charles Carter, Richard Layard,
Peter Venables, Gareth Williams

The 1970s will be a decade of exceptional challenge and opportunity
in higher education. As talents that previously lay idle or wasted
knock at the doors of colleges and universities in unprecedented
numbers, the imagination and variety of courses, and the standards
and flexibility of institutes that offer them, will be tested to the full.
Decisions must be made now on how to provide an education that
can be judged, whatever its academic or vocational flavour, by its
contribution to the quality of the civilization we inherit and live
through, at a cost that allows the job to be properly done.

Many voices will contribute to the debate on choice and decision,
but few with the authority and realism that the authors of this book
offer. From different viewpoints they give alternative appreciations
that both clarify the wide range of issues involved, and face the
reader with the questions that, at a turning-point in the evolution
of a democratic society (for the opening up of education beyond
school is nothing less), every teacher, parent and student must
confront and resolve for himself.

George Brosan is Director of the North-East London Polytechnic,
and was formerly Principal of Enfield College of Technology

Charles Carter is Vice-Chancellor of the University of Lancaster

Richard Layard is Lecturer in Economics and Deputy Director of
the Higher Education Research Unit at the London School of
Economics

Peter Venables was formerly Vice-Chancellor of the University
of Aston

Gareth Williams is Associate Director of the Higher Education
Research Unit at the London School of Economics